ROUGHSHOD THROUGH DIXIE

Grierson's Raid 1863

DESTROYING THE RAILROAD.

MARK LARDAS

First published in Great Britain in 2010 by Osprey Publishing,
Midland House, West Way, Botley, Oxford, OX2 0PH, UK
44–02 23rd St, Suite 219, Long Island City, NY 11101, USA
E-mail: info@ospreypublishing.com

Print ISBN: 978 1 84603 993 5
PDF e-book ISBN: 978 1 84603 994 2

Page layout by: Bounford.com, Cambridge, UK
Index by Margaret Vaudrey
Typeset in Sabon
Maps by Bounford.com, Cambridge, UK
3D BEVs by Alan Gilliland
Originated by PPS Grasmere Ltd, Leeds, UK
Printed in China through Worldprint

10 11 12 13 14   10 9 8 7 6 5 4 3 2 1

A CIP catalog record for this book is available from the British Library

THE WOODLAND TRUST

Osprey Publishing is supporting the Woodland Trust, the UK's leading
woodland conservation charity, by funding the dedication of trees.

AUTHOR'S ACKNOWLEDGMENTS

I would like to thank Jane Evans, the librarian at the Enterprise Public
Library, who generously provided her time to obtain archival materials
about the appearance of Enterprise, Mississippi at the time of the
American Civil War. I would also like to thank Kay Jorgenson of *The
Artilleryman* magazine, and Jim Bender for help with information about
and a photo of the Woodruff gun.

AUTHOR'S NOTE

The following abbreviations indicate the sources of the illustrations used
in this volume:

MOA – The Making of America Archives, Cornell University
LOC – Library of Congress, Washington, D.C.
AC – Author's Collection
Other sources are listed in full.

DEDICATION

This book is dedicated to my friends at the Helen Hall Library in League
City, TX. Librarians are a researcher's best friends.

FOR A CATALOGUE OF ALL BOOKS PUBLISHED BY OSPREY MILITARY
AND AVIATION PLEASE CONTACT:

Osprey Direct, c/o Random House Distribution Center,
400 Hahn Road, Westminster, MD 21157
Email: uscustomerservice@ospreypublishing.com

Osprey Direct, The Book Service Ltd, Distribution Centre,
Colchester Road, Frating Green, Colchester, Essex, CO7 7DW
E-mail: customerservice@ospreypublishing.com

www.ospreypublishing.com

CONTENTS

INTRODUCTION

The Union patrol rode cautiously north of Baton Rouge. It was May 2, 1863. Earlier that day, pickets outside Baton Rouge had stopped a sleeping cavalryman that approached their lines. The man claimed to be an officer from an Illinois cavalry regiment. But there were no Illinois units in the Union Army's Department of the Gulf. Those regiments came from Massachusetts or New York, with a few Louisiana regiments raised from local loyalists. The rider had spun a wild story, claiming that his brigade had ridden the length of Mississippi, from Tennessee to Louisiana.

He convinced the officer commanding Union forces in Baton Rouge, General Christopher Auger, there was something behind his story. Confederate forces north of the line held by Union forces in Louisiana were moving around frantically. Something had stirred them up. Wild rumors were flying around.

Auger sent two companies of cavalry to investigate under Capitan Godfrey of the First Louisiana Cavalry (US). As they approached a plantation in the debatable ground between the lines, Godfrey saw a colonel come out of the plantation house, waving a handkerchief. The colonel introduced himself as Benjamin Grierson, commanding the First Brigade of the Cavalry Division, Army of the Tennessee.

The previous night the unit had broken through the last Confederate forces between the brigade and Union-held Baton Rouge. Rather than risk blundering into friendly fire, Grierson halted the march at the plantation, three miles from the Confederate and six miles from the Union lines. Scouts sent to make contact with Union forces included the unfortunate orderly who had fallen asleep, to be carried to the Union pickets by his horse.

It was hardly surprising that the man had fallen asleep. The brigade had spent 16 days behind enemy lines, and spent virtually the last 32 hours awake in the saddle. They were dead on their feet. While waiting for representatives from Auger's garrison, Grierson, a former music teacher and band leader, kept himself awake by playing a piano in the parlor of the plantation house.

As a result of the raid Benjamin Grierson became a celebrity in the North. Here a front-page illustration that appeared in *Harpers Weekly* depicts a highly romanticized Grierson as a cavalier. (LOC)

HARPER'S WEEKLY.
A JOURNAL OF CIVILIZATION

Vol. VII—No. [...] | NEW YORK, SATURDAY, JUNE 6, 1863 | [SINGLE COPY ... / ... PER YEAR ...]

COLONEL GRIERSON, SIXTH ILLINOIS CAVALRY.—FROM A PHOTOGRAPH BY JACOBY, OF NEW ORLEANS.—[SEE PAGE 364.]

Godfrey still initially found the story Grierson related hard to credit. Grierson, the two cavalry regiments with him, and a battery of light guns, had started from La Grange, Tennessee. The various detachments had ridden through over 600 miles of Confederate territory, destroyed 50 to 60 miles of railroad tracks, several bridges and culverts, and cut telegraph lines at numerous places. Yet Gibson was soon convinced. Grierson and his men had come from Illinois – their accent made that clear. There was also a lot of physical evidence. In addition to the Illinois troopers, the column had nearly 1000 runaway black slaves, over 30 vehicles, from buggies to lumber wagons, and 400 Confederate prisoners. As well, Grierson's force had 800 more horses and mules than it had started with, collected over the length of Mississippi.

For now, Grierson and his men wanted nothing more than to sleep. It was a wish that was to be deferred. When they finally reached Baton Rouge, General Auger insisted on a victory parade.

Grierson's men made an impromptu parade through the streets of Baton Rouge. They wore their travel-stained uniforms, so muddy and dusty that it was hard to tell to which army they belonged. Many of the troopers had exchanged uniforms for civilian clothing and hats along the way – they had left La Grange with no spare clothing. But the men were cheered by hastily gathered crowds, and serenaded by the regimental bands of the city's garrison.

The Sixth Illinois Cavalry led the parade, followed by the artillery, the Confederate prisoners, and the Seventh Illinois Cavalry. Behind the soldiers came the runaway blacks, leading the horses captured in the raid. The wheeled vehicles taken brought up the rear, driven by more runaways.

When Grierson and his men finally arrived at Baton Rouge, most had not slept since dawn, May 1. They were persuaded to parade through the town before they ate and finally rested. (MOA)

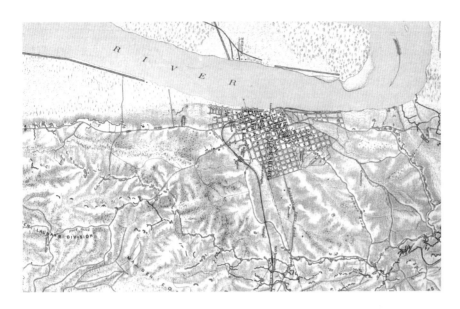

Vicksburg and its defenses.

The brigade was finally allowed to sleep. When they woke up the next morning, they discovered that they had become national heroes. Benjamin Grierson and his First Cavalry Brigade had just presented the Union cause with a victory – the first clear victory after a frustrating six months filled with defeat and stalemate. Grierson and his men had caught the imagination of the North, and Grierson became a hero of the illustrated press. He was lionized as a new Achilles. His brigade was fêted through Louisiana, honors followed, and a promised yet long-delayed promotion to brigadier general finally came through.

Perhaps the celebration struck Grierson, a modest non-drinker with a diffident temperament, as excessive. Certainly he was frustrated by the immediate aftermath of the raid. Grierson wanted a swift return to the Army of the Tennessee's cavalry division. One of the brigade's three regiments was back at La Grange, having been detached to draw off pursuing Confederates. Instead, Nathaniel Banks, commanding the Department of the Gulf, hung on to Grierson's troopers as if they were a lucky talisman. It would be months before Grierson's brigade was reunited.

Yet the excessive celebration, the honors – even Banks' view of the brigade as a good-luck piece – were understandable. Grierson's Raid was the most successful Union cavalry raid of the Civil War – possibly the most successful on either side. For not only had Grierson's brigade cut through Mississippi, but also pursuit of the column had drawn off thousands of Confederate troops in Tennessee, Mississippi, Louisiana, and Alabama.

While the rebels were vainly seeking Grierson, Ulysses Grant moved his army south of Vicksburg, landing at Grand Gulf. By the time the distracted Confederates could turn their attention to the real threat – Grant's Army of the Tennessee – it was solidly positioned on the Mississippi's east bank, impossible to dislodge. From there Grant would march north and invest Vicksburg, capturing it on July 4, 1863. Grierson's Raid was not only materially successful, but it achieved its overarching strategic objective.

ORIGINS

Raid, ride, and road share a common root. In Old and Middle English the words were often interchangeable. George MacDonald Fraser used that ambiguity in the title of his novel *The Candlemass Road* – about a border raid that took place on Candlemass Day. To ride was to raid. By the twentieth century the term "raid" defined a pinpoint strike with fixed objectives, intricately planned and meticulously timed. Yet the classic cavalry raids of the American Civil War used the older meaning of the word "raid." A Civil War cavalry raid was less a choreographed precision strike than a thing of loose objectives and improvisation.

Cavalry served three major functions in the Civil War – reconnaissance, security, and mobility. It was used to scout out the location of the enemy; to seize critical pieces of terrain, holding it until infantry could reinforce it; and to counter enemy reconnaissance and attempts to seize terrain.

Cavalry was also used to strike deep into enemy territory, to destroy supplies and transportation. Civil War armies were of a size unprecedented in America. They consisted of tens of thousands of men – occasionally in excess of 100,000 soldiers – with accompanying draft animals and baggage trains. A strike against vulnerable supply lines and depots could force an army to retreat without battle. Grant had been forced to withdraw his troops probing toward Vicksburg after Confederate cavalry under General Earl Van Dorn raided and destroyed his supply depot at Holly Springs, Mississippi.

J. E. B. Stuart, Robert E. Lee's commander of cavalry in the Confederate Army of Northern Virginia, was a master at employing cavalry to confuse the enemy about Lee's intentions. Stuart's ride around General George McClellan's Army of the Potomac in September 1862 not only struck at McClellan's supply lines, it served to demoralize Union forces, undermined McClellan's reputation with his superiors, and forced the Yankee army to commit more troops to guard their rear, and send fewer to the front.

A cavalry raid served to focus enemy attention on the raiders, and distract attention away from a campaign's main thrust. Stuart's first ride around the Army of the Potomac, during the Peninsular campaign in June 1863, served no real military purpose, but it unnerved McClellan, distracting his attention from the main Confederate army at a critical point during the battle. John Hunt Morgan and his Confederate cavalry struck deep into Kentucky from Tennessee in July 1863, ultimately crossing the Ohio River into Indiana. While unsuccessful in drawing forces away from Grant, besieging Vicksburg or General George Meade's Army of the Potomac (then chasing Lee in Pennsylvania), the raid forced the Union's Army of the Cumberland to react. This delayed the Union push to Knoxville.

Improvisation was inherent in the nature of a Civil War cavalry raid. Any deep raid balanced on a knife's edge between triumph and ignominy. Cavalry moved fast, but lacked both hitting power and staying power. Infantry firing rifled muskets outranged cavalry firing carbines. In prepared positions, on steady ground, regular infantry fire would not only be more accurate than mounted men firing from horseback, but had greater effect, since they fired a heavier, harder-hitting ball.

Yet militia or garrison soldiers – the troops cavalry raiders were most likely to encounter during a raid – often threw away those advantages due to a lack of discipline, readiness, or steadiness. If charged before they could

A contemporary painting of a Civil War Union cavalryman by Edwin Forbes. Forbes was employed by Frank Leslie's *Illustrated Weekly*, the Civil War's version of the television news. (LOC)

organize, they often scattered. If cavalry, however, hesitated or gave them time to coalesce, they could be as dangerous as regulars. A successful raid depended upon a commander's ability to know when to attack immediately and when to withdraw instantly.

A successful commander also had to recognize when an opportunity presented itself unexpectedly or when what seemed to be an opportunity was instead a trap. Had the intended target departed early, leaving the objective barren? What did you do if you came across an unscheduled pack train? Should you take the time to re-provision your unit from the captured supplies or destroy them and move on? When did you rest your men and horses and when was it more important to press on despite fatigue? These and numerous other questions arose during any raid. Guess right and you became a hero. Guess wrong and your command would be trapped, with surrender and disgrace to follow.

Critical to success was continued movement. As long as a column was on the move, the enemy could not concentrate upon it. Lose momentum and you could lose your entire command, as one enemy unit pinned you down and others surrounded you while deep in enemy territory, without hope of resupply or reinforcement. Successful commanders knew how to maintain progress, while misleading the opposition about their intentions.

At first, the Civil War cavalry raid seemed wholly owned by the Confederate States of America. Men like Stuart and Morgan, as well as other outstanding Confederate cavalry leaders like Bedford Forrest and John Singleton Mosby virtually defined cavalry and the cavalry raid during the Civil War. There were several reasons for greater Confederate success with cavalry than that experienced by the Union, especially at the outset of the war.

The Confederate states were more agricultural than the urbanized states of the Union. Goods could travel by water year-round in most of the South, reducing dependency on roads. The Southern road network was less developed than that of the North. A larger percentage of the Confederacy's population was rural, and the bad roads meant that travel was best done on horseback.

In the North, a much larger percentage of the population was urban. If you traveled by horse at all in the city, you rode in a carriage, on a horse-drawn streetcar, or at the reins of a wagon, hauling goods. Northern winters also made water travel problematic and so goods were moved by sledge or wagon. There was a need for more and better roads. That meant that even in the summer, Northern farmers were more likely to be traveling by wagon than on horseback. This gave the South a much larger pool of trained riders to draw upon at the war's onset.

There was also a cultural advantage. Southern society was more aristocratic than that of the North, with the average Southern white male viewing himself as a cavalier, an heir to the chivalrous knight. The cult of the horse was greater in the South too. Equine sports, such as racing, were more developed, and stock breeding – including race horses – played a larger part in the lives of the Southern gentry.

While two-thirds of all West Point graduates that saw service during the Civil War remained loyal to the Union, this ratio was reversed with cavalry officers. Nearly 60 percent of the United States Army's cavalry officers resigned their commissions when the Civil War began, and served in the Confederate army. This leadership edge gave Southern cavalry another initial advantage over Northern troopers at the start of the war.

A final advantage possessed by the South was problems with initial cavalry doctrine in the Union Army. At first the Northern army viewed cavalry as a source of pickets, guards, messengers, and orderlies. Cavalry was closely tied to the army, and deployed in small, decentralized units. It was not until after the first year of the war that the Union began fielding cavalry in divisional units, and centralizing cavalry's use.

By 1863 Union cavalry had made significant qualitative strides. Doctrine had improved, albeit mainly as a reaction to Confederate success. A year or more of experience with horses had turned Yankee cavalrymen – even those initially unfamiliar with riding – into horsemen. The Union's superior logistic and organizational skills began to tell. While Confederate cavalrymen were expected to bring their own mounts, the Northern Army supplied the horses. By the start of 1863 the Union's acquisition and breeding programs were beginning to give Union horsemen superior mounts.

Even more importantly, the Union was beginning to develop cavalry officers that could match their Southern counterparts. Commanding cavalry was as much an art as a science and great cavalry officers were born, not made. Some of the most gifted cavalry officers in the Civil War – on both sides – had little or no prewar experience with cavalry. Bedford Forrest had been a slave trader, Mosby a lawyer, and Morgan a merchant. Philip Sheridan and James H. Wilson, two of the most successful Union cavalry leaders, had been officers before the war, but Sheridan had been an infantryman and Wilson an engineer.

In 1863, New Year's Day was primarily noted as the day Lincoln's Emancipation Proclamation would take legal force. But it also marked another change: it was the year that Yankee cavalry would mature. While Sheridan and Wilson's achievements as cavalrymen lay in the future, even as 1862 ended Benjamin Grierson's reputation was emerging. His achievements had already attracted the attention of his superiors, who marked him as the right type of man to lead a deep cavalry raid.

Before the year was half over, not only would a Union cavalry unit conduct a successful raid, it would do it on a scale that surpassed Confederate achievements.

INITIAL STRATEGY

By early spring of 1863 General Ulysses S. Grant and the Union's Army of the Tennessee had been trying to take Vicksburg for over six months. Grant had attempted to take the city from the north, and the east. The navy had steamed up the Mississippi River from New Orleans to attack the city from the west. Each attempt had been stymied, most recently a December attempt by William T. Sherman's XV Corps to capture Vicksburg via Hayne's Bluff, north of Vicksburg.

After that repulse, Grant decided that the only way to fully invest Vicksburg would be to attack it from the south, landing an army on the eastern bank of the Mississippi River, then cutting north. This approach offered two challenges: landing the army safely, and then supplying it.

In March Grant finally solved the supply problem. Initially he tried to find a route around Vicksburg using a combination of canals and bayous as a water bypass, but that had failed. He then used one of his corps to build a road on the Louisiana side of the Mississippi, running from Milliken's Bend to Hard Times. He could march an army on it – and move the ammunition and military supplies that the army would require by pack and wagon trains. These could be in position at Hard Times by the middle of April – supplies and men enough to hold a beachhead on the Mississippi side of the river.

This road did not allow Grant to move enough food and forage to feed the army, but Mississippi south of Vicksburg was farmland. In April and May the granaries, smokehouses and storehouses along the route would still hold enough to provide the food and fodder his army would need. Further, the spring harvest, which came early in the South, would offer still more food and forage.

Grant's proposal was contingent upon having the Union naval forces on the Mississippi River south of Vicksburg. The Union warships would control the Mississippi between the Confederate strongholds at Vicksburg and Port Hudson, and the transports would ferry men and supplies across the river. But David D. Porter, not Ulysses Grant, commanded United States Navy forces on the upper Mississippi.

Taking the fleet south was a major risk. They could run Vicksburg's batteries going downstream but attempting to return north, against the current, would be so slow that the batteries would almost certainly destroy the fleet. Once Porter's ships were south of Vicksburg, they were inexorably committed. Until and unless Vicksburg fell, the Union navy would be cut off from its bases in Missouri and Tennessee.

Grant enjoyed good relations with Porter. It is a measure of Porter's faith in Grant that Porter committed his command on Grant's assurance of success. Porter agreed to run the Vicksburg batteries with his flotilla and on a moonless night in mid-April he slipped past Vicksburg's guns. Despite careful Confederate preparations – including bonfires on the Louisiana side to illuminate targets – Porter was successful. Only one ship, the transport *Henry Clay*, was sunk. Damage to the rest of his force was minor.

Grant could now move an army across the Mississippi River south of Vicksburg. The one remaining obstacle was landing it safely. General John Pemberton commanded Confederate forces in the state of Mississippi. Pemberton had enough men to adequately garrison Vicksburg, and maintain a large enough field force to drive an invader crossing the Mississippi River back into the water as it landed. Once Grant was ashore and established, he could rebuff any such Confederate attempt, but while the army was landing it would be tremendously vulnerable.

To distract Confederate attentions away from his proposed landing sites, Grant decided to use misdirection. He would first focus Confederate attention well north of Vicksburg with two feints. Both involved Sherman's Corps. The first, conducted a month before Grant's intended landing date, involved landing the Corps' First Division, commanded by General Frederick Steele, near Greenville, 100 miles north of Vicksburg. Operating in northern Mississippi, the unit would focus Confederate attention above Vicksburg. It would be withdrawn after a few weeks, but not until Pemberton had committed additional troops to the Yazoo Delta, well away from the Grand Gulf–Port Gibson area where Grant intended to land.

Next, a few days before Grant moved General John A. McClernand's XIII Corps and General James McPherson's XVII Corps from the Louisiana to the Mississippi side of the river near Hard Times, Sherman would land at Hayne's Bluff. Sherman had attempted to capture Vicksburg along that route in December, and had been repulsed. Grant felt that Pemberton would take a second assault in that direction seriously. This time Sherman did not intend

FEBRUARY 7 1863

Raid proposed by General Ulysses S. Grant

Vicksburg was the prize sought by the Union and defended by the Confederacy. It is shown as it appeared from the deck of a Union warship during the Civil War. (AC)

to attack; he would land his corps, deploy for battle, and wait. Once Grant established the Army of the Tennessee firmly in Mississippi south of Vicksburg, Sherman would re-embark his men, land them in Louisiana, then march them south of Vicksburg, where they would rejoin Grant.

With luck these operations would draw Pemberton's forces to Vicksburg and north of the city. However, there were plenty of reserve troops scattered around the state of Mississippi as well as in neighboring Alabama. Most were infantry. The bulk of Pemberton's cavalry – 6,000 men under Earl Van Dorn – had been sent to Tennessee in late winter 1862 to help General Braxton Bragg fight the Army of the Cumberland. Despite this, Pemberton had more than enough troops south of Vicksburg to stall any move by Grant across the Mississippi River long enough for help to arrive from Vicksburg.

As long as the railroad network across the state of Mississippi remained intact, reinforcements could also be rushed in from Alabama, or even

General Ulysses Grant was the architect of the successful plan to take Vicksburg. He suggested a cavalry raid against the Southern Railroad to be led by Grierson as early as February 1863. He is shown here at the siege of Vicksburg. (LOC)

Tennessee and Georgia. Three sets of tracks influenced Grant's planned offensive. The Southern Railroad of Mississippi (later known as the Alabama and Vicksburg Railroad) ran east–west across Mississippi from Meridian to Vicksburg. It was the main supply route to Vicksburg. The New Orleans and Jackson, which became the Mississippi Central at Jackson, Mississippi, ran north–south through the center of Mississippi, eventually reaching Memphis, Tennessee. (Later it formed part of the Illinois Central Railroad.) The Mobile and Ohio (later known as the Gulf, Mobile, and Ohio) roughly paralleled the Mississippi Central north and south along the eastern Mississippi.

Disrupting any of these railroads, but particularly the Southern of Mississippi, would assist Grant greatly. The ideal means of doing this would be a cavalry raid, especially one aimed against the Southern. Grant had begun exploring the idea in February, suggesting to General Hurlbut, who then commanded at Memphis, that a raid to cut the railroad east of Jackson, Mississippi "would prove a great damage to Vicksburg." Such a raid would also have the added benefit of distracting attention away from the Mississippi River. Grant originally proposed using a picked force of 500 men. This was the size of a cavalry regiment, large enough to reach the railroad, yet small enough that if it were subsequently lost, it would not seriously weaken the Army of the Tennessee.

Success depended upon finding the right unit and the right commander for the raid. By March, Hurlbut had his man – Colonel Benjamin Grierson – along with Grierson's command, the First Brigade of the Cavalry Division. It comprised three volunteer cavalry regiments – the Sixth Illinois Cavalry, the Seventh Illinois Cavalry, and the Second Iowa Cavalry.

The three regiments were typical of the cavalry of the Union's western armies. All had been raised from volunteers living in America's heartland – the prairies of Illinois and Central Plains of Iowa. These men thought of themselves as men of the West, even if their Confederate opponents called them Yankees. To those that lived in the prairies and plains, a Yankee was someone from New England, not Illinois or Iowa. Unlike the cavalry regiments raised in the Union states of the Eastern Seaboard, these units had no shortage of capable riders. Most men volunteering to join these units were farmers, or men from the small towns of America's plains.

When organized, these regiments each had 1000 men, divided into ten 100-man companies. In April 1863, eighteen months after being raised and after nearly a year of combat, all three were below authorized strength. The Second Iowa had between 600 and 700 men, the Sixth Illinois around 500, and the Seventh Illinois approximately 550. While well below the numbers prescribed in the table of organization, the regiments were the average size of those actually on field service.

A year's hard service had scoured these regiments of the incompetent, the unlucky, and the lazy. The men who remained had been taught in the hard school of combat. They had been fighting Confederate cavalry – both regular units and the bewildering assortment of partisan, ranger and other mounted irregulars and guerrillas in Missouri, Tennessee, and Mississippi.

The Sixth Illinois Cavalry had been raised in November 1861. Its commander was Lieutenant Colonel Ruben Loomis, who had joined the regiment as a captain when it formed, and moved steadily up the ranks. Loomis achieved command after Benjamin Grierson, the previous colonel, was promoted to brigade commander. During the period it had been commanded by Grierson, the Sixth Illinois had chased guerrillas for six months in the border region of Kentucky and Tennessee during 1862, before being transferred to the Department of the Tennessee in September. Since then, along with the usual scouts, it had participated in Grant's Central Mississippi campaign.

The Seventh Illinois Cavalry was being led by Colonel Edward Prince. A lawyer before the war, Prince had joined the regiment when it was raised in October 1861. His prewar interest in cavalry led to his appointment as cavalry drill master, with the rank of lieutenant colonel. He succeeded to command in 1862. The regiment had spent a year fighting along both sides of the Mississippi River, seeing extensive action in both Missouri and Tennessee. In December it was brigaded with the Sixth Illinois and Second Iowa under the overall command of Benjamin Grierson.

The Second Iowa was the oldest of the three regiments, albeit by only a few months. It had been raised at Davenport, Iowa, in August 1861. Since then it had seen a significant amount of fighting in both Missouri and Tennessee. In April 1863, it was commanded by Colonel Edward Hatch.

Hatch had been a lumber dealer in Iowa prior to the war, but was visiting Washington D.C. when the Civil War started. He had been one of the civilians volunteering to guard the White House from secessionists. Rushing back to Iowa, he joined the Second Iowa when it formed, as a captain. By June 1862 he had been promoted to colonel, and was commanding his regiment. Like Grierson, Hatch was a man with no prior experience with the military but who proved to be an outstanding cavalry commander.

The three regiments had been amalgamated into a brigade in November 1862 under the command of Colonel Benjamin Grierson. Grierson had started with the Sixth Illinois Cavalry as a major. His competence was noted, and he soon moved up, replacing the regiment's original colonel – an indolent and incompetent officer who owed his position to political connections rather than aptitude. Not that political connections were viewed as a bad thing by Grierson and many other Civil War officers. Grierson had been part of the Illinois Republican machine before the war, and owed his commission more to abolitionist politics than to prior military experience. But Grierson proved to have an aptitude for cavalry command. His regiment had distinguished itself under his command, and by April 1863 he commanded the cavalry brigade to which the Sixth Illinois belonged, as well as his own regiment. His promotion to brigadier general was overdue.

Since its formation, the brigade had participated in Grant's abortive campaign in central Mississippi, spending the first three months of 1863 crossing sabers with Confederate cavalry in southern Tennessee. As a result, Grierson was already marked for bigger things. When Grant had written to

Hurlbut in February, Grierson was the man Grant wanted to lead the proposed raid. But Grant had added, "I do not direct that it be done but leave it for a volunteer enterprise."

The opportunity suited Grierson. He longed for an independent command where he could use his cavalry to best advantage, unfettered by less capable superiors. In December 1862, during Grant's offensive in central Mississippi, Grierson twice had to break off his brigade's pursuit of Van Dorn's cavalry when his orders from Grant were overridden by General Charles S. Hamilton, then Grierson's superior. Indeed, at one point Grierson had his brigade taken away from him and given to one of Hamilton's favorites. Only Grant's personal intervention had restored Grierson to command.

Since then, Grant had reorganized the army. Grierson's brigade was now in General Sooy Smith's Cavalry Division. Smith recognized Grierson's abilities, and used Grierson as his wheel horse. However Smith was an uninspired commander, moving cavalry too slowly for Grierson's taste – or for much success. The raid was the type of chance Grierson had sought, and he willingly volunteered to lead it.

A strike against the Southern Railroad would take a Union force deep into the territory of the Confederate Department of Mississippi and Eastern Louisiana. Headed by General John C. Pemberton, the department consisted of the state of Mississippi and Louisiana east of the Mississippi River. Pemberton had nearly 45,000 men under his command scattered throughout the department. Additionally, Pemberton could detach a regiment or two of infantry as blocking force, without seriously weakening Vicksburg.

The largest part of Pemberton's command, including Stephenson's and Smith's division, was concentrated at Vicksburg. In all, these forces totaled almost 23,000 men, although on March 31, 1863, only 16,000 were present for duty. Most of this garrison were slow-moving infantry or artillery and were required to protect Vicksburg from attack. Pemberton had two on-call cavalry units – Wirt Adams' Mississippi Cavalry Regiment and the Waul's Texas Legion Cavalry Battalion, the combined force led by Wirt Adams.

Adams, originally from Kentucky, had drifted to Texas when it was a republic, and had served in the Texas army in 1839, fighting Indians there. He had moved to Mississippi in 1850 and became a successful banker and planter. When the Civil War started Adams had been offered the position of Confederate Postmaster General, but declined. Instead he took a cavalry commission, and proved a resolute and competent cavalry leader. With a combined strength of around 15 companies, Adam's command served as Pemberton's rapid reaction force in Vicksburg.

Another brigade, Green's, was stationed at the Big Black River, where the Southern Railroad bridged the Big Black. It was made up of Arkansas and Missouri troops, infantry and dismounted cavalry (fighting as infantry), along with two batteries of artillery. It had an aggregate strength of 2,500 men. As with the infantry at Vicksburg, these troops would have the greatest utility along Mississippi's railroads.

While infantry on foot was too slow to catch a fast-moving cavalry raid, it could be mounted to increase mobility. Moved by railroad, it could guard the lines upon which they were moving, serving as the anvil to pin down Yankee cavalry long enough for Confederate cavalry to hammer the raiders into surrender.

Down at Grand Gulf was Brigadier General John S. Bowen's brigade, with nearly 3,000 men, made up of Missouri infantry, with supporting artillery. It also had a company of Louisiana heavy artillery. These guns were intended to control the Mississippi River. Bowen's brigade would have its attention focused on the river, but it too had enough strength to crush a raiding cavalry brigade foolish enough to attack it.

Further south, guarding Port Hudson, Louisiana, was Franklin Gardner's command. With 20,000 men, it was the second-strongest Confederate force in the department. It consisted of five infantry brigades, three heavy artillery battalions, and a collection of cavalry organized in independent companies and battalions. In all, Gardner could probably field 1200 or so mounted men. As with Vicksburg, except for the cavalry, the majority of these troops were required to garrison Port Hudson.

Pennsylvania-born John Pemberton went South at the start of the Civil War, allying with his adopted home. At the time of Grierson's Raid, Pemberton commanded the Confederate Department of Mississippi and Eastern Louisiana, and coordinated the counterthrusts against Grierson. (LOC)

In northern Mississippi there were three concentrations of troops. The bulk of General William Loring's division was garrisoning Fort Pemberton, near Greenwood, Mississippi, with detachments at Canton and Jackson. This force was intended to check any Union movement toward Vicksburg via the Yazoo River. It had over 8,800 men present, although only three-quarters of the force was ready for active duty. It had little cavalry – only one regiment of Tennessee cavalry – perhaps 400 men. The rest of the division, mostly infantry, was used to moving quickly, however. In many ways, this division represented the department's fire brigade. The division was 40 miles from the Mississippi Central Railroad at Winona, but could reach it with a day and a half's hard marching. In mid-April one brigade, Buford's, was ordered to Bragg's command in Tennessee. It was scattered on trains across Mississippi when Grierson's Raid began.

Further north, at Panola County, was Brigadier General James Chalmers with 800 cavalrymen. This force was intended to screen northern Mississippi

BENJAMIN GRIERSON

Benjamin Grierson in 1863. (LOC)

Benjamin Grierson, the leader of Grierson's Raid, was an unlikely warrior. The son of Irish immigrants, he was born in Pittsburgh, Pennsylvania in 1826, the youngest of six surviving children. His father, Richard, was a successful merchant and shoemaker. Disliking Pittsburgh, and sensing greater opportunity to the west, Richard moved the family to Youngstown, Ohio, when Benjamin was three. Benjamin's earliest memories were of growing up in rural Youngstown.

When Benjamin was eight he almost died after being kicked in the face by a horse. He remained in a coma for almost two weeks, but eventually recovered. The incident had two permanent results. It made him distrustful of horses thereafter, and left a prominent scar on his face. He concealed the scar with his trademark beard when he was old enough to do so.

Grierson proved a musical prodigy. He mastered several instruments, among them flute, clarinet, piano, violin, and drum, and was playing with the Youngstown Band even as a child. By the time he was 13 he was elected the band's leader. After he graduated from Youngstown Academy he pursued a musical career. He wrote music (a collection of which was assembled and published in 1998), led a band, and taught music.

However, Grierson abandoned music in the early 1850s. He and his family had moved to Jacksonville, Illinois, in 1849, lured by the promise of cheap, fertile land. Frontier Illinois was too thinly populated to give Grierson a steady income through teaching music or leading bands. Additionally, he wished to marry his childhood sweetheart, Alice Kirk, whose father would not consent to a marriage unless Grierson could provide for her. Grierson married Alice in 1854.

In 1856 he entered into partnership with John Walihan, a successful shopkeeper in Meredosia, Illinois, running a general store. The store prospered for the first two years, but the Panic of 1857 set the business on a path to bankruptcy. The partners had bought stock on credit to expand their inventory during the booming days of 1856 and, due to the panic, customers could not pay for goods. Caught in a cash-flow crunch, Walihan and Grierson went bust in early 1861. It left Grierson with a heavy debt burden that would take years to pay off.

At the same time, the Union was dissolving. With the outbreak of the Civil War, Grierson decided that his duty lay in fighting to preserve his country. He was a staunch

from the Army of the Tennessee. Grierson's brigade had matched forces with these men on several occasions.

Headquartered at Columbus, Mississippi, was Daniel Ruggles, with 2,300 men. Ruggles was responsible for the defense of northeastern Mississippi – from Pontotoc County eastwards. Most of Ruggles' command – perhaps two-thirds – were cavalry. This included the 22nd Tennessee Cavalry Regiment under Colonel Clark Barteau. Barteau had been born and raised in Ohio, but had moved to Tennessee in 1855. There he started a newspaper and taught. He soon became an opponent of the abolitionist

abolitionist, the result of the influence of both his parents and his father-in-law, John Kirk, who had been a leading abolition figure since the 1840s. Attracted by its Free Soil plank, Grierson had been active in the Republican Party from its inception in 1856. He was friends with Illinois governor Richard Yates, and soon received an appointment as aide-de-camp to Benjamin Prentiss, who was in charge of Illinois state troops.

Grierson acted as Prentiss' aide for six months. The position was unpaid, yet he remained despite his unpaid debts and the objections of his wife. Finally, on October 24, 1861, Governor Yates appointed Grierson as a major. The commission was in Grierson's least-desired branch – as an officer of the Sixth Illinois Volunteer Cavalry. Grierson took it, beginning a remarkable career as a cavalryman.

Grierson soon learned the rudiments of cavalry tactics, and became the most competent officer in his new regiment. This included the regiment's commander, T. M. Cavanaugh. Cavanaugh, another political appointment, was frequently absent and uninterested in duty when he was present. As a result, the regiment was unready for duty in early 1862. Finally, 37 regimental officers – not including Grierson – petitioned Yates to remove Cavanaugh and replace him with Grierson; Cavanaugh resigned. Grierson was promoted to colonel, and made regimental commander.

Under Grierson, the regiment prospered. It earned a reputation for aggression and competence in Kentucky and Tennessee, soon becoming known as Grierson's Cavalry. Having gained the favorable attention of General Sherman, Grierson was given a brigade when the Sixth Illinois was moved to the Army of the Tennessee, and trusted with the execution of the most ambitious cavalry raid attempted by the Union army.

After the conclusion of Grierson's Raid, Grierson received an overdue promotion to brigadier general in the volunteers, and spent a frustrating year under the command of senior officers of limited competence who treated Grierson and his brigade as a lucky talisman. Nathaniel Banks hung on to Grierson's brigade until July 1863.

Once back with the Army of the Tennessee, Grierson was subordinate to Sooy Smith, who was Grierson's inferior when it came to handling cavalry. In February 1364 Grierson participated in a poorly managed cavalry raid by Smith, which moved too slowly and indecisively. It opened Tennessee to a raid by Bedford Forrest, which culminated in the Fort Pillow massacre, and tarnished Grierson's reputation. It was not until December 1864 that Grierson was allowed another independent raid. Also through northern Mississippi, that raid was another brilliant success.

Following the end of the Civil War, Congress authorized creation of four black regiments – which became known as "the Buffalo Soldiers." Grierson was offered a regular army commission as colonel, and command of the Tenth Cavalry. He accepted. The pay offered an opportunity to repay debts doing a job that he enjoyed and at which he was competent. He served in the Army for the next 24 years, in positions of increasing responsibility. Grierson was promoted to brigadier general in April 1890, and retired in July of that year.

His first wife, Alice, died in 1888 and Grierson remarried in 1897 to Lillian Atwood King. Following retirement, he moved back to Jacksonville, Illinois, although he also had homes in Fort Concho and Michigan. He suffered a debilitating stroke in 1907, and finally died on August 31, 1911 at his vacation home in Michigan.

movement, joining a Tennessee regiment when the Civil War started. Barteau's cavalry was another force with which Grierson's men had frequently fought – and would fight again.

Finally, at Jackson, Mississippi, Brigadier General John Adams had 500 men to guard the state capitol and railroad junction. Jackson was a major army depot and the most important rail junction in the state. While the fixed garrison at Jackson was small, it could call out a significant amount of the local population for home defense. Reinforcements could quickly be rushed via railroad as well.

Rolling stock was crucial to supplying large numbers of troops in the field during the American Civil War. The Confederacy never had enough, and each boxcar burned by Union raiders represented a reduction of Confederate logistics capabilities. (LOC)

These were not the only troops a raiding force needed to worry about. Given a day's warning, most towns in Mississippi could muster a militia force of 100 to 300 men. While these militia troops were poorly disciplined, and armed with hunting rifles and shotguns, each encounter would produce delay and casualties. While no single encounter with a militia unit was likely to defeat regular cavalry, the cumulative effect of a dozen to a score of such battles could weaken a raiding force to the point where it would be easy prey for an intercepting regular Confederate unit.

Additionally, in an emergency Pemberton could draw reinforcements from neighboring departments. The Department of the Eastern Gulf had some 6,000 men near Mobile, Alabama, and a day's journey on the Mobile and Ohio Railroad could bring enough men to Meridian to crush a cavalry brigade. Bedford Forrest had another large cavalry force in Alabama, which could sweep into eastern Mississippi with the same ease that it cut through central Tennessee and Kentucky.

There was also a sizable Confederate army in Tennessee under Braxton Bragg, threatening the Union's Army of the Cumberland. Bragg's army included 6,000 cavalry led by General Earl Van Dorn, and 8,700 under the command of John Hunt Morgan. In January, Van Dorn and 3,400 cavalrymen had been transferred from Pemberton's command to help Bragg's offensive. This left Pemberton almost denuded of mounted men. Pemberton had been demanding Van Dorn's return since then.

A successful Union raid into Mississippi might convince General Joe Johnston, commanding Confederate forces in the West, to heed Pemberton. If that happened, Grierson might find himself with a parallel situation to his experience in late 1862. Instead of chasing Van Dorn's raiders, Grierson would be pursued by Van Dorn.

Finally, if a raid were viewed with sufficient alarm in Richmond, the Confederate capitol, raiders could face even more serious opposition.

The railroads that formed Grierson's primary objective were a wild card in the game. They offered mobility that even mounted cavalry could not match. Even given the slow speeds at which trains had to travel on the poorly maintained southern tracks, a train could move 300 miles in one day.

A train pulling 15 boxcars could move 1,000 infantrymen in full kit, albeit in crowded conditions. With a flatcar and a stock car substituted for two boxcars, an average-sized infantry regiment with 700 men could bring two artillery pieces with gunners, caissons carriage, and horses. More infantry could be moved if the artillerymen found local draft animals to pull the guns. A battery of cannon supported by infantry was force enough to deter a cavalry brigade.

The Vicksburg campaign provided an illustration of the mobility offered by rail. After Grant landed at Port Hudson on May 1 and began moving towards Vicksburg, Richmond ordered a brigade rushed from Charleston, South Carolina, to reinforce Joe Johnston's relief expedition. Regiments that left Charleston by late May were available by early June. The brigade moved to Savannah, Georgia, on the Atlantic coast – again by train – in August.

It was a formidable number of troops for a single cavalry brigade to challenge, yet had Grierson known the actual numbers opposing him it would have encouraged him. Like McClellan in the East, Grant in the West overestimated the size of the Confederate army. Grant's estimates were 50 percent higher than the number of men actually available and fit for duty in Pemberton's department. Unlike McClellan, Grant was undeterred by his estimate of Confederate capability. The only effect the overestimation of Pemberton's force had was to increase the importance of any distraction caused by a raid against the Southern Railroad.

THE PLAN

Between February 7, when what would become known as Grierson's Raid was proposed, and its execution in mid-April, a plan evolved for the raid. It was the result of a collaboration of several levels of command. Grant provided the strategic focus of the raid, and the timing of its beginning. He wanted the Southern Railroad cut between Meridian and Jackson, and he wanted it cut a week before he began moving the Army of the Tennessee across the Mississippi River. This would not only delay supplies from reaching Vicksburg prior to its investiture, but would also distract Confederate attention at a critical time, and prevent Pemberton from reinforcing any troops opposing Grant's landing.

When the raid was first proposed, its effects on Vicksburg were almost secondary. At that time Grant intended to swing south first after landing in central Mississippi to capture Port Hudson. Then the Army of the Tennessee, reinforced by General Nathaniel Banks' Army of the Gulf would move north to Vicksburg. The joint army would be supplied via the Mississippi River. General Bank's dilatoriness forced Grant to revise his plan to the one executed in 1863, but that change occurred after the raid began. It did not alter the raid's strategic objectives however.

Turning a strategic objective into a practicable operation was a challenge. Actual planning for the raid was split between Hurlbut, Sooy Smith, commanding the cavalry division, and Benjamin Grierson, the raid commander. The plan that resulted was primarily Grierson's, with Hurlbut and Smith providing such resources that fell outside a cavalry brigade.

The 1860 model light cavalry saber issued to Union cavalry in the American Civil War. (US Army Heritage and Education Center)

Grierson's brigade was stationed at La Grange, Tennessee, well north of the Southern Railroad of Mississippi. Reaching the railroad would require an overland penetration some 250 miles, deep into Mississippi. Today that distance can be traveled in five hours by automobile. On horseback, a mounted formation would account itself fortunate to reach that distance in five days, especially given the primitive roads in mid-19th-century Mississippi.

Traveling by road in enemy territory invites both attention and ambush. Avoiding roads whenever possible made a raiding force less detectable and less predictable, especially during the approach to the objective. Avoiding roads was safer, but took longer. A minimum of a week's hard ride was allocated to reach the Southern line. That meant the raid should start two weeks before Grant's intended crossing date.

The size of the raid and the forces to be employed were next determined. Grant originally envisioned committing Grierson with 500 men, and felt that the Sixth Illinois by itself was sufficient. Hurlbut and Grierson, with Smith's concurrence, increased the raiding force to include all of Grierson's current command, the First Brigade of the Cavalry Division. That gave Grierson a force of 1,750 cavalry troopers. The capabilities of these individual troopers were critical to the raid, and carefully considered in its planning. For combat, each cavalryman was equipped with a carbine, a revolver, and a saber.

The two Illinois regiments and four companies of the Second Iowa used Sharps carbines, a standard Union cavalry carbine. It was 39½ inches long (1.003 meters), weighed eight pounds (3.629kg) and fired a .52-caliber (.535 inches or 13.6mm) bullet. It was breech-loading and rifled. The Sharps made before and during the Civil War had a vertical sliding breechblock. They used paper cartridges, but could be loaded with black powder if the user lacked cartridges. However, this ability to use loose powder was balanced by the size of the round. A standard infantry musket of the day fired a .58-caliber round, which would not fit in a Sharps barrel.

Because they were breech-loading, Sharps rifles could be fired prone, from behind cover or from horseback. The primer was built into the cartridges so firing it was as simple as sliding the cartridge into the chamber, closing the breech, aiming the rifle, and pulling the trigger. An experienced cavalryman – and after a year of combat, Grierson's men were experienced – could fire ten rounds a minute. The Sharps had a range of about 1000 yards. Stephen Forbes, when a private in the Seventh Illinois, wrote home stating that he could kill a man "at half a mile" with his. While this was theoretically possible, its effective range was more likely to be 300 yards.

Six companies of the Second Iowa used the Colt Repeating Carbine, a rifle-length version of the Colt six-shooter. The army version hit the market in 1855. Colt made several varieties of the rifle, including carbines. The Second Iowa most likely had the .44-caliber version. If so, they could use the same ammunition for both their carbines and their pistols. The .44-caliber Colt Repeating Carbine had six cylinders and a barrel that was around 32 inches (0.812m) in length. It weighed a little over seven pounds (3.18kg).

The Colt Carbine was not a breech-loader. Like the Colt pistols, it used a paper cartridge, loaded from the front of the cylinder. Reloading was involved and time-consuming, unsuited to a hot firefight. In some units soldiers paired off in combat, with one man firing one carbine while another reloaded the second.

Each cylinder had to be carefully sealed with grease when reloading, or risk a shot causing the other bullets to fire simultaneously. Since the left hand supported the barrel ahead of the cylinder, this type of misfire shot the user's fingers off. The Colt was also delicate, a combination that led to the regular army rejecting the weapon, and its unpopularity with some soldiers. However, as a repeating rifle it gave users a lot of firepower, and obviously several hundred had been available when the regiment was forming.

Despite its short length of carbines, the Colt was often awkward to fire while mounted and on the move. For that, a cavalryman carried a pistol, and there were a variety of these used by Union cavalry forces. It is likely that the men in Grierson's brigade were issued with some version of the Colt Army Revolver, a .44-caliber pistol with six cylinders. While some troopers may have had different pistols, the ones they were most likely to have been issued with were either the 1848 Colt Dragoon or the 1860 Colt Army Model. The army purchased 127,000 1860 Army Colts, most during the Civil War.

The Dragoon weighed 4 pounds 4 ounces (1.93kg) and was 14¾ inches (374mm) long, with a 7½-inch (190mm) barrel. The 1860 Colt weighed 2 pounds 11 ounces (1.22kg), and had a 14-inch (355.6mm) overall length when fitted with the standard 8-inch (203mm) barrel. Both fired a .44-caliber bullet that weighed nearly a third of an ounce (9.4g), and was accurate to about 100 yards. The gun also used a paper cartridge, loaded from the front of the cylinder. A loaded revolver could be fired six times in as little as six seconds. Again, reloading the pistol was an involved and time-consuming process, unsuited to a firefight. Experienced troopers were therefore sparing with fire, preferring to make each shot tell as opposed to firing for effect. While soldiers were issued one revolver, some obtained a second – just in case.

Finally, a cavalryman had a saber. While many Eastern cavalry units soon discarded their sabers, the Western cavalry kept theirs. The saber was better as a weapon of intimidation than for any real military utility. It was harder for inexperienced troops to stand up to the swinging edge of a saber than the muzzle of a revolver. The threat offered by the saber seemed more personal. Experienced infantry was less likely to be cowed, but no smart cavalryman wanted to charge experienced and prepared infantry, anyway.

By 1863, there were two versions of the saber issued to Union cavalry – the Model 1840 cavalry saber and the Model 1860. The 1840 saber was 44 inches (1.12m) long, with a 35-inch (0.89m) blade, and weighed six pounds (2.72kg). The 1860 saber, known as the "light" cavalry saber, was 41 inches (1.04m) long, with a 33-inch (0.84m) blade that was 1 inch in width. It weighted 3 pounds 9 ounces (1.70kg). Both had curved blades, with the sharpened edge on the convex side, and were intended as slashing weapons.

The 1860 saber, significantly lighter and handier than the earlier model, was better adapted to cavalry fighting during the Civil War. It had only just gone into production when the three regiments in Grierson's brigade were raised, so these men were probably initially issued one of the 24,000 1840 sabers manufactured before they ceased production in 1858. The Seventh Illinois almost certainly was equipped with the 1840 sabers, as the regiment had been raised as a result of an arms dealer selling the army sabers that he had found forgotten in a Missouri armory. A photograph of Stephen Forbes taken in 1861 shows him posing with an 1840 saber. However, it is likely that troopers took the opportunity to replace the "wristbreaker" 1840 sabers with the lighter 1860 model.

A horse gave a cavalryman mobility. By 1863 most fighting was done dismounted, especially against infantry. Mounted confrontations generally occurred only when cavalry met cavalry, or when attacking militia and unprepared infantry. If you caught enemy soldiers in camp or on the march, or encountered a baggage or supply train, you charged mounted, depending upon pistol and saber. Otherwise, you dismounted and fought behind cover, taking advantage of the ability to reload a breech-loader while lying down.

There was a chronic shortage of suitable cavalry mounts in the armies of the Tennessee and Cumberland in the first half of 1863. Grierson had more troopers than horses, and the horses that his men did have were often unsatisfactory – spavined, blown, or infirm. While his regiment had received a draft of horses in March, most were unsatisfactory. As a result, many men were mounted on inferior horses. Other troopers rode into Mississippi mounted on Tennessee mules – one creature of which the state had a sufficiency. Grierson was not unduly worried about the available horseflesh. Horses were bred in Mississippi, especially northern Mississippi. Grierson knew that by the time the brigade reached its goal all of his men would be adequately mounted – courtesy of those in rebellion against the United States.

To further increase the chances of success, Battery K of the First Illinois Artillery was added to the raid. It was a horse artillery unit, equipped with six light Woodruff guns. These guns were among the most unusual pieces of ordinance in the Union Army. They were intended as "galloper guns" – field pieces to accompany mounted cavalry. The barrel weighed just 256 pounds (116kg), and it had a 2-inch (50mm) bore. The guns fired a conical 2-pound (0.9kg) lead round. It was a sort of oversized Minié ball. Alternatively, the gun could be loaded with cased 1-ounce (28g) lead shot.

The gun was mounted on a special carriage made by a manufacturer of civilian buggies and wagons in Quincy, Illinois, which also made the caissons. The piece was light enough to keep up with cavalry when pulled by two horses. The carriage was fragile though, and tended to break under hard usage.

They were the invention of James Woodruff, an Illinois manufacturer with dreams of achieving martial glory through ordinance. Feeling that the army lacked an artillery piece suitable as horse artillery, he filled the gap with this iron gun – to be manufactured at his Quincy, Illinois, factory. The army turned down the new weapon however. It weighed more than the existing brass

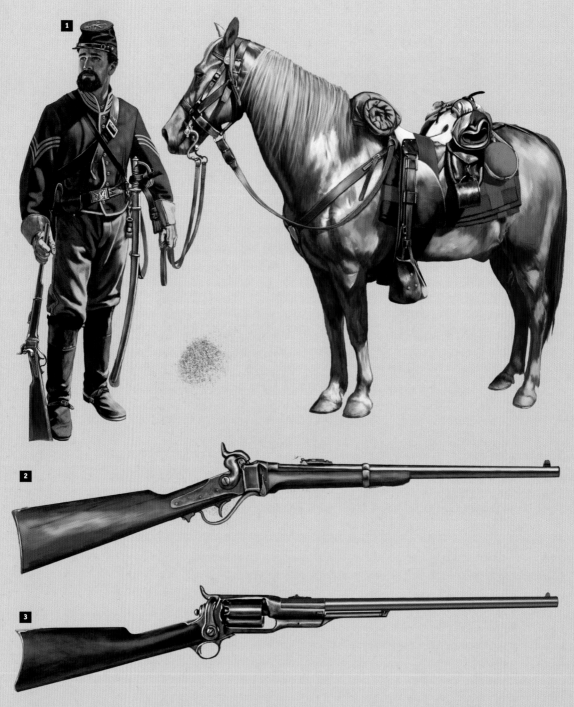

Grierson believed in traveling light. The troopers that accompanied his raid were equipped as seen here **1**. A bare minimum of kit was carried: their personal weapons, five days rations including double salt (with the understanding that the rations were to last ten days), and forty rounds of ammunition per firearm. In addition to their carbine and pistol, the troopers carried a saber. The Sixth and Seventh Illinois and part of the Second Iowa were equipped with Sharps cabines **2**. The rest of the Second Iowa carried Colt's Revolving Rifles **3**.

12-pound (5.4kg) howitzer and had only three-quarters the range of that piece. Further, it used non-standard ammunition that would complicate logistics.

Woodruff was well connected politically within the Illinois Republican Party and used his influence with Abraham Lincoln to get the decision reversed. Woodruff also sweetened the pot by offering to sell the army 9,000 sabers, 1,500 Colt revolvers, and 1,500 carbines that he had located, if he received a contract to manufacture the Woodruff gun. The army's need for cavalry weapons was great and the cost of a limited number of Woodruff guns was trivial. So the army signed a contract for a trial order of 30 guns in 1861. If the guns proved useful more orders would follow. If not, the army received enough weapons to outfit an additional cavalry brigade.

The Army Ordinance Board's assessment of the gun's utility proved accurate. Woodruff's guns were useful so long as there was no other artillery in the field. The 30 guns delivered were scattered among various Iowa, Illinois, and Missouri regiments. Their value proved limited, one battery using its Woodruff guns as carts with which to remove their dead from the battlefield. But Grierson saw something in the guns, and wanted them along. As it turned out, they proved highly useful during the course of the raid.

The next issue was *where* to cut the line. A major objective of the raid was to serve as a distraction. Anonymously destroying a length of track in the Mississippi countryside, and slipping away silently, would not achieve that goal. A town along the route would be the best objective. Hitting a town would not only offer an opportunity to destroy track, but also the depot facilities associated with a railroad. Locomotives needed water and fuel to run, and got both at small stations along the route.

The six Woodruff guns that accompanied the raid provided critical support at decisive points in the raid. This Woodruff gun is a park monument in an Illinois city today. Its carriage is not the same type used with Woodruff guns during the Civil War, but rather the standard Civil War artillery carriage. (Photo courtesy Jim Bender)

Meridian was possibly garrisoned, and a larger town than desirable for a raiding brigade. It was a possibility, but not a good first choice. Other options included Hickory, Newton, Lake, Forest, and Morton – all whistle-stop villages along the Southern Railroad. Newton and Forest were the best choices of these, as they were scheduled watering spots for the steam locomotives. Newton had an additional advantage, as it was closer to the north–south Gulf and Ohio Railroad.

While Grierson's primary objective was the Southern, disabling the Gulf and Ohio would also be beneficial. It was also a natural target for a Union cavalry raid – more so than the more distant Southern. Moving parallel to the Gulf and Ohio as he drove into Mississippi achieved two things: it gave Grierson's Confederate opponents a focus for their attention that was removed from his actual goal; and, if Grierson got lucky, he might get an opportunity to actually hit the Gulf and Ohio, as well as the Southern. Newton became Grierson's principal objective as a result.

Sooy Smith was Grierson's immediate superior at the start of the raid, and led one of the diversionary raids that helped Grierson penetrate deep into Mississippi. He is show here in a postwar photograph. (LOC)

A rough outline of an approach route began to coalesce. Grierson's route would run from La Grange, Tennessee to Pontotoc, Mississippi. At that point it would appear to be a standard Union cavalry scout of northern Mississippi, possibly with an attempt to collect Confederate horses. This was a good way to disguise the ultimate purpose of the raid. Union cavalry in western Tennessee was chronically short of good mounts in early 1863. Northern Mississippi was one of the Confederacy's sources of mounts. Remounting Union horsemen on Confederate mounts simultaneously strengthened the Northern armies while weakening the Confederacy's cavalry.

Grierson's superiors had other plans to disguise his intentions. The Army of the Tennessee would launch two other scouts on the same day that Grierson started his raid. Sooy Smith would lead one raid, taking command of some 1,500 men from five infantry regiments, supported by artillery. This column would push into northwest Mississippi from La Grange along the route of the Mississippi Central Railroad. A second force, with 1300 men, would advance into Mississippi from Memphis along the Mississippi and Tennessee Railroad.

These raids were to be short, shallow penetrations into Mississippi. While the infantry in the two supporting raids could not hope to catch Chalmers' fast-moving cavalry, these two pushes – seemingly converging at Granada, where the two railroads met – would focus Chalmers' attention on the threat posed to Vicksburg by an offensive down the Mississippi Central axis. It might even draw Loring's forces north, away from both Grand Gulf and Newton.

The Confederates would also be prevented from concentrating on a single Union effort; they had to counter all three raids. Each raid, including Grierson's critical effort, would face less opposition than it would if only one penetration were attempted. Three raids would split the attention of Confederate forces in northern Mississippi. Flooding the zone with Union forces along a broad front increased the probability that Grierson and his men could slip south undetected amid the confusion.

There would be a further distraction to Confederate attentions. General Rosencrans, commanding the Army of the Cumberland in central and eastern Tennessee, planned his own raid into Confederate soil. Led by Colonel Abel Streight, it was to sweep through northern Alabama and Georgia. The two armies decided to coordinate the start of both raids to further divide the attention of Confederate cavalry.

Once Grierson was past the screening Confederate cavalry, he could stay ahead of them by riding hard and fast. No other Confederate cavalry would be between Grierson and the Southern Railroad. Grierson would cut south through Mississippi, roughly following a line from Pontotoc, through Houston, Starkville, Louisville, Philadelphia, and Decatur to Newton. Along the way Grierson could make lunges east, against the Gulf and Ohio. If he encountered resistance, he would continue south. If he did not, he would destroy track on the Gulf and Ohio. Either way, he got closer to his real goal.

This route was only an outline. Circumstances could force alterations. If he got ahead of his opposition, he would take to the roads and race south.

If he ran into trouble, he would break contact, probably by going to the west, and then ride cross country. If he found a welcoming committee in the form of regular infantry in one of the towns – including Newton – he would break off and hit the railroad where Confederate troops were not.

Along the way he would destroy any bridges he crossed, if this could be done without incurring a significant delay. In the short term this would slow pursuit of Grierson's brigade. In the long run, it would make moving troops through Mississippi more difficult until the bridges were repaired. This would slow any reaction against Grant. Finally, Grierson's men would cut any telegraph lines they encountered. It only took a few minutes' work to pull down a line and cut a length of wire. That cut communications, delaying pursuit and sowing confusion.

Taking the cut wire away and disposing of it at a remote location – preferably in a river or pond – further delayed repair of the telegraph line. It would not be enough for a repair crew to locate the break – difficult enough when a line ran through miles of swamp, woods, or fields – and splice it. A repair crew would have to replace the missing line. By 1863 telegraph line was a scarce commodity in the Confederacy.

Once at Newton – or whatever town the raiders ultimately reached – the cavalrymen would do as much damage to track and town as time permitted. There were strict rules as to what could or could not be deliberately destroyed. Most government buildings were fair game, although medical facilities such as hospitals were exempt. Industrial buildings with military application could also be destroyed.

This rule had a wider scope than those buildings devoted to the production of weapons. A shoe factory or clothing mill could be burned because it could supply uniforms to the army. Whether or not that plant had actually sold goods to the military, it could in the future. Any metalworking or blacksmith's shop was a legitimate target because of its potential to repair or produce weapons. So were any buildings or facilities associated with a railroad, due to the extensive military use of them. Stocks of food and fodder beyond the level of personal subsistence were also fair game, to deny their use to enemy armies.

There were limits. A hotel used as a barracks could be burned, but not typically a private dwelling. Personal property was supposed to be inviolate. Government mails were legitimate booty, but personal mail was supposed to be left alone. Livestock and vehicles could also be taken as they had military value.

In 1863 livestock included human beings – black slaves. Slaves were still considered property in the United States. However, slaves owned by those in rebellion against the United States had been considered "contraband of war" since May 1861, because slave labor could be used to aid the rebellion. The Emancipation Proclamation, which came into force on January 1, 1863, went further, declaring slaves in territories in rebellion against the United States as free men. However, except where Union forces – such as a raiding cavalry brigade – could enforce it, the proclamation was a dead letter in those territories.

These rules were frequently more honored in the breach than in observance during the Civil War, and cavalrymen were notorious for

Telegraph lines were vital to communications and vulnerable to damage. Grierson's raiders rarely had time to chop down or damage telegraph poles, but they frequently cut long lengths of wire, and dumped the cut wire into ponds or streams. (LOC)

"foraging" forbidden items – money, watches, jewelry, and other valuables – from civilians, and burning down civilian barns and homes. Grierson intended to follow these rules. There was a large dose of self-interest in his doing so. His success depended upon speed, and cavalrymen overloaded with plunder could not move quickly. An acquiescent population secure in their property if they left the raiding troopers alone was less likely to hinder Grierson's movements than a people outraged at having their homes torched.

Another consideration was a desire not to unduly alienate the civilian population. There was believed to be significant Union sentiment in rural Mississippi and several of the rural counties had voted against secession in 1861. Grierson hoped to fan that loyalty into renewed support for the United States by using a gentle hand.

Finally, there was a time factor. Destruction took time. Grierson planned on stopping at Newton – or whatever his objective proved to be – for the minimum possible time. He planned for no more than twelve hours, and that was barely long enough to destroy legitimate military contraband. Grierson wanted to do all of the damage he could in as short a period, and leave.

That left the final and fuzziest part of the raid's plan – the withdrawal. At that point, if everything went as planned, Grierson and his men would be deep in Mississippi. Once Grierson's presence was known, he could expect Confederate units throughout Mississippi to converge upon him. And, in these days before radio, he had no way of getting help from Union forces upon his return. He would be strictly on his own.

The least likely way out would be the way he came. To the north would be a string of angry Mississippi civilians and Confederate soldiers stirred up by his passage. Instead the plan called for Grierson to cut east, south of Meridian, cross into Alabama, and then hook through the northwest corner of Alabama. From there he could slip back into Mississippi around Corinth, and then back to Tennessee and home. One advantage of this plan was that it provided yet another crack at the Gulf and Ohio Railroad.

Alternatively he could ride west and south to Grand Gulf or Port Hudson. By the time Grierson and his men were approaching the Mississippi, Grant would be ashore, and he and Grierson could rendezvous. The risk in this approach lay in the uncertainty of knowing exactly when and where Grant would land. There was also a sizable Confederate garrison at Grand Gulf and circumstances could delay Grant. If so, Grierson could get pinned between hostile Confederate forces at Grand Gulf and the Mississippi River, or get trapped between Grand Gulf and Confederate forces transferred from Jackson or Vicksburg. To reach Grand Gulf or Port Gibson from Newton would require a ride of 150 miles or so, as Grierson would have to take a roundabout path to avoid Jackson and Vicksburg.

Another possibility was to ride to Natchez, take the town, and depend upon the navy to evacuate the brigade. It could be done, as there was no

Soldiers of the Second Tennessee Cavalry Regiment. This unit was part of Clark Barteau's command that chased Grierson's brigade to Houston, Mississippi, and then was decoyed into following Hatch's Second Iowa north. (AC)

permanent garrison in Natchez. The problem was attracting the attention of the navy with enough time to organize a mini-Dunkirk before the Confederates could crush Grierson's brigade.

A final route was one that was then considered the least likely – continue southwest through Mississippi and into Louisiana. From there, Grierson and his men could link up with Nathaniel Banks' Department of the Gulf. The route was long, and there were the dangers associated with making contact with the Union army – a different army than Grant's. Grant was holding knowledge of the raid closely due to security concerns. The closest large Union garrison was at Baton Rouge. This was another 200 to 250 miles, depending upon how circuitous Grierson made the path.

Grierson's superiors were sympathetic to the problems associated with his escape. The orders they issued essentially gave Grierson permission to do whatever he wanted, and take whichever path looked most promising for escape. Smith also planned a series of cavalry and infantry sweeps across northern Mississippi a week after he heard that Grierson had reached the Southern Railroad, in the hope that it might aid Grierson's escape.

Regardless of how he got in and got out, Grierson planned on moving fast and that meant traveling light. The brigade went on the raid with a bare minimum of equipment. Every excess piece of kit was left at La Grange. Troopers brought their weapons, 40 rounds of ammunition for their carbines and revolvers, oats in the feedbags for the mounts, five days' rations in haversacks for the men, and a double ration of salt. Everyone was made to understand that rations were to last ten days.

Grierson intended to feed his mounts and men off the land, and to collect as many remounts as possible, seizing food, fodder, and horses from those Mississippians supporting the rebellion. Grierson had no plans to carry away either wagons or (despite his abolitionist sympathies) runaway slaves for fear that these items would slow his progress. Similarly, Grierson intended to avoid combat as much as possible, riding around trouble whenever it was an option. Forty rounds per firearm could be expended in two hot engagements, leaving him unarmed deep in enemy territory without means to fight his way out.

To navigate, Grierson had two items – a pocket compass and Colton's pocket map of Mississippi. Afterward he noted that Colton's map "though small, was very correct."

THE RAID

APRIL 17 1863

The raid begins

Grierson almost missed the raid he planned, as it was delayed with Grant's offensive. As the Mississippi Raid continued to hang fire, Grierson applied for overdue home leave. On April 3 he was ordered to carry dispatches to Springfield, Illinois, allowing him to visit his home. Grierson was in Jacksonville, Illinois, when Hurlbut ordered Sooy Smith to prepare to launch the raid. Hurlbut telegraphed Grierson to return at once. Grierson did so, arriving in Memphis at midnight on April 17. Hatch had the brigade mounted and ready to go at 3:00 am. Had Grierson been any later, the resulting effort might have become "Hatch's Raid."

The actual departure was delayed because Smith wanted to confer with Grierson. In addition to cutting the Southern Railroad, Smith gave Grierson verbal instructions to use one regiment to cut the Mississippi Central near Oxford, and a second to cut the Mobile and Ohio near Tupelo, with the usual caveat of "if practicable." Grierson's brigade and supporting artillery rode out of La Grange at dawn, heading southeast. The men had gathered through barracks telegraph that they were "going on a big scout to Columbus, to play smash with the railroads." The only two members of the raid that knew the actual objective and plan were Grierson and his aide, Lieutenant Samuel L. Woodson.

The raid began in excellent conditions. The weather was fair and sunny as the brigade rode southeast to Pontotoc. The first day's march covered nearly 30 miles, with the brigade camping that night at the Ellis Plantation, four miles northwest of Ripley, Mississippi. Little resistance or even enemy contact was experienced during this day. There was a brief skirmish with five or six Confederate soldiers in which three were captured. Another Mississippian, a civilian who was driving an ox team, had a hat "which one of the boys took a fancy to, and relieved him." Colonel Prince, commanding the offending Seventh Illinois, compensated the robbed man by paying $2 in Union greenbacks.

At this point the Confederates were only just discovering that a raid had started. Additionally their attention was divided. Streight was already in

APRIL 18 1863

The brigade crosses the Tallahatchie River at New Albany

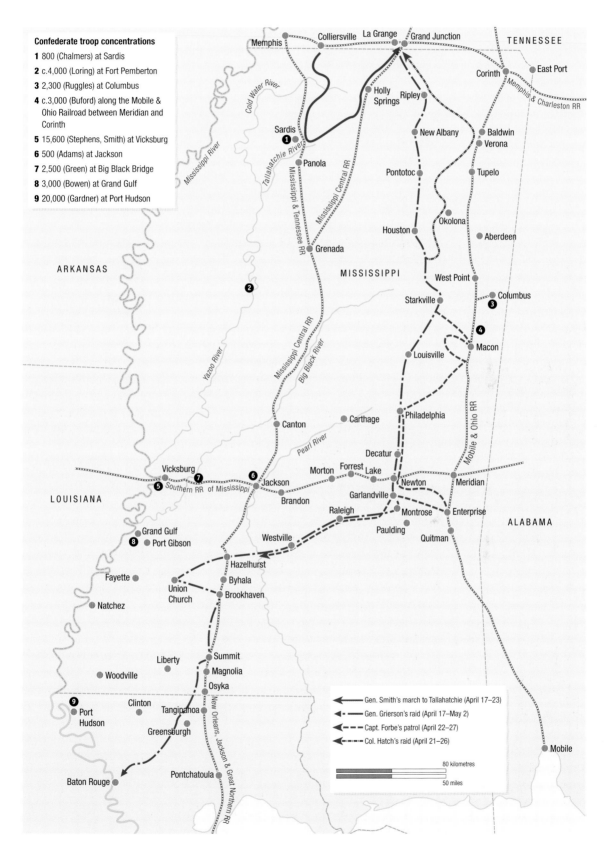

Confederate troop concentrations

1 800 (Chalmers) at Sardis

2 c.4,000 (Loring) at Fort Pemberton

3 2,300 (Ruggles) at Columbus

4 c.3,000 (Buford) along the Mobile &
Ohio Railroad between Meridian and
Corinth

5 15,600 (Stephens, Smith) at Vicksburg

6 500 (Adams) at Jackson

7 2,500 (Green) at Big Black Bridge

8 3,000 (Bowen) at Grand Gulf

9 20,000 (Gardner) at Port Hudson

TENNESSEE

Memphis · Colliersville · La Grange · Grand Junction

Corinth · East Port

Memphis & Charleston RR

Holly Springs · Ripley

Sardis **1**

New Albany · Baldwin · Verona

Panola

Pontotoc · Tupelo

Mississippi Central RR

Cold Water River

Tallahatchie River

Mississippi & Tennessee RR

Mississippi River

Houston · Okolona · Aberdeen

ARKANSAS

Grenada

MISSISSIPPI

West Point · Columbus **3**

2

Starkville

4 Macon

Louisville

Yazoo River

Mississippi Central RR

Big Black River

Philadelphia

Mobile & Ohio RR

Canton · Carthage

Pearl River

Decatur

Vicksburg **7** · Morton · Forrest · Lake · Newton · Meridian

5 · Jackson · Southern RR of Mississippi

6 · Brandon · Garlandville

LOUISIANA · Raleigh · Montrose · Enterprise

Paulding

ALABAMA

Grand Gulf **8** · Port Gibson · Westville · Quitman

Fayette · Hazelhurst · Byhala

Union Church · Brookhaven

Natchez

Summit

Liberty · Magnolia

Woodville · Osyka

9 Port Hudson · Clinton · Tanginahoa

Greensburgh

New Orleans, Jackson & Great Northern RR

Baton Rouge · Pontchatoula

Mobile

→ Gen. Smith's march to Tallahatchie (April 17–23)

◄—— Gen. Grierson's raid (April 17–May 2)

◄- - - Capt. Forbes's patrol (April 22–27)

◄-·-·- Col. Hatch's raid (April 21–26)

80 kilometres

50 miles

northern Alabama along with a large infantry force commanded by General Grenville Dodge, while Smith was taking an infantry brigade – initially by railroad – down the Mississippi Central line towards the Tallahatchie River.

Second Day – April 18

At 7:00 am the brigade mounted up and headed southeast. The weather was again excellent. As the on the first day, little enemy contact was made. The brigade passed through Ripley at 8:00 am, and crossed the Tallahatchie River at three places near New Albany. There they encountered light resistance. The Seventh Illinois sent one battalion to capture a bridge at New Albany. They encountered a few Confederate skirmishers there and drove them off. An advance company was sent forward to the bridge, where they found a picket attempting to destroy it. These men were driven off and the battalion crossed over the bridge. The rest of the Seventh as well as the Sixth Illinois crossed at a ford, two miles upstream at Arizabee, while the Second Iowa forded four miles west of that. The brigade reunited in New Albany, at 5:00 pm, then camped for the night at Sloan's Plantation, five miles south of New Albany.

By the second day, the Confederates were starting to react to the raid. Chalmers was engaged with Smith's column. Additionally, he became aware of a new Yankee probe – this one down the Mississippi and Tennessee Railroad. As a result only Ruggles' First District troops were available to intercept Grierson; Chalmers was too busy. Ruggles sent Barteau's cavalry scouting for Grierson's men. A patrol of Barteau's men were the troops that made contact with the Yanks north of New Albany, and picketed the bridge. Word of the Yankee presence soon worked its way to Barteau, but he was still uncertain as to the raid's size or Grierson's intentions.

Third Day – April 19

The fair weather with which the raid began had disappeared by April 19. Rain began bucketing down after sunset on April 18, and persisted throughout the night. It continued rainy for the next few days. This would work to Grierson's advantage: the rain limited visibility. While it slowed Grierson, it slowed his opposition too. Grierson also knew where he was and where he was going, while they did not. Further, Grierson had some general idea where his opponents were.

To confuse pursuit, Grierson broke up his regiment at the start of April 19. He sent one detachment of the Seventh Illinois back to New Albany, the Second Iowa to Chesterville, Mississippi, to the southeast, and another northwestward to King's Bridge. The object of these moves was to behave as if the purpose of the raid was to attack Confederate cavalry camps in northeast Mississippi. The King's Bridge thrust came up empty, as the troops there belonged to Chalmers' command and had left to deal with Smith. They brought word to Grierson that the Confederates had burned the Mississippi Central bridge at the Tallahatchie River. Grierson felt this news meant that railroad was cut close enough to Oxford to satisfy that portion of his orders. Thereafter his attention was focused south and east.

At New Albany the Seventh Illinois flushed out 20 Confederates, and killed or wounded eight. After these morning feints the brigade converged at Pontotoc, which the Sixth Illinois reached first, at 4:00 pm. They met light resistance. One Confederate militiaman was shot and killed while sniping at the Union troops. Another squad of militia in Pontonac fled at the approach of the cavalry. They left behind a wagon, loaded with ammunition and camping equipment, which was destroyed.

The Seventh Illinois brought up the rear, as they had been seeking horses along the way. They failed to find horses, but when they stopped for dinner, some "foraging" troopers found a cache of weapons and gunpowder in one of the houses along the route. Against orders, the finders "accidentally" burned the house. Another detachment of the Seventh Illinois came across 500 bushels of salt owned by the Confederate government. This too was destroyed.

After riding through Pontotoc, the brigade camped at two plantations five miles south of Pontotoc – Weatherall's and Daggett's on the road to Houston. After they had camped, Grierson inspected his command. He selected 175 men who he felt were incapable of hard riding, as well as the worst horses. By this time the brigade had managed to capture a sufficient number of first-class remounts to replace the inadequate horses and mules. The unfit men and beasts were collected into a provisional battalion and placed under the command of Major Hiram Love of the Second Iowa. Grierson also assigned one of his six Woodruff guns to this unit – which the rest of the brigade dubbed "the Quinine Brigade."

The Sixth and Seventh Illinois Cavalry in march order. This photograph was taken by a Confederate agent in Baton Rouge and shows Grierson's brigade at the end of their raid. (AC)

On the third day of the
raid, Grierson's brigade
camped at Weatherall's
plantation south of
Pontotoc. This plantation
was owned by the brother
of the man who
commanded Confederate
state forces in the area.
(MOA)

Fourth Day – April 20

Grierson detached the Quinine Brigade from his command soon after midnight on April 20. They were ordered to return to La Grange, and give the impression that they contained the entire raiding force. This was Grierson's first attempt to deceive the Confederates as to the intended depth of the raid. With luck, they would follow Love's detachment, thinking it was Grierson's brigade.

Love did his best to help the deception. He started north at 3:00 am, marching in columns of four to produce the illusion that he had a full regiment. The riders took all of the Confederate prisoners with them, and led spare horses and mules, further increasing the number of northbound hoof prints. They rode through Pontotoc to ensure that they would be spotted moving north. Love also had the lone Woodruff gun wheeled back and forth over the same ground to leave four sets of tracks.

Two hours later, at 5:00 am, Grierson led the rest of his brigade south, toward Houston, Mississippi. He reached Houston at 4:00 pm, but then he moved off the road, and traveled cross country around Houston. From there he pushed south another 12 miles toward Clear Springs, halting for the night at the plantation of Benjamin Kilgore. In all, the brigade had ridden over 40 miles in one day.

Grierson failed in his objective of convincing the Confederates that he was heading back north, however. His ride around Houston had been noticed, and locals had sent word to Colonel Clark Barteau, commanding Ruggles' cavalry. At this point, Barteau's cavalry was the only force that could catch Grierson, and he was riding hard in pursuit. The reports received

exaggerated Grierson's strength, so Barteau wanted to find and fix Grierson, holding him until more help arrived. There was help at hand, as Buford's brigade of Loring's division was in the process of being transferred to Tennessee. It was strung out along the Gulf and Ohio, where the regiments were halted to await developments.

Fifth Day – April 21

Grierson had a raider's instincts, and decisions he made on the 21st proved it. He felt uneasy about the success of the deception attempted with the Quinine Brigade. He sensed rather than knew that he was still being closely pursued, and decided that a larger diversion was needed. Grierson decided to detach an entire regiment. Before leaving camp he had arranged for the Second Iowa to strike east towards the Gulf and Ohio.

Grierson chose the Second Iowa for this independent mission based on several factors. Its commander, Edward Hatch, was Grierson's most senior regimental commander, as well as his most talented subordinate. The Second Iowa was his largest unit. It started the raid with 700 men, and still had over 500 even after the culling at New Albany. Finally, it was the only unit equipped with repeating rifles. It could maintain a heavier rate of fire, but would run out of ammunition faster. The detached regiment would return to La Grange sooner, which would allow the Second to use its rifles to best advantage.

Hatch was unhappy at the prospect of being sent off, and even less happy when, due to a mix-up in orders, the brigade broke camp and headed southeast at 6:00 am rather than the intended 3:00 am. Two hours later, when the brigade reached the road junction where roads led to West Point, Columbus, and Louisville, Hatch, the Second Iowa and one of the five remaining Woodruff guns took the road to Columbus. Grierson with the rest of the command followed the Louisville road.

Hatch had been ordered to strike the Gulf and Ohio, destroying the railroad from West Point to Macon, then to cut north, burn Columbus, and return to La Grange. These orders proved overly ambitious, but the tracks the Second Iowa made toward West Point decoyed Barteau and the rest of the Confederates away from Grierson.

Barteau and his cavalry had been chasing Grierson since April 18. On April 21 Barteau's men were thundering southwest after Grierson and rode into Kilgore's plantation around 10:00 am. His scouts moved south following Grierson's tracks. It was still raining hard. At the road junction, they saw two sets of tracks – one heading south and one heading east. Grierson had taken the precaution of having one battalion of the Second accompany him south for a while before doubling back in columns of fours.

Barteau's scouts saw the fresher tracks headed north and then east. Hatch had also run his Woodruff gun back and forth, leaving four sets of tracks. Barteau and his men assumed that all the Yankee raiders had doubled back then headed east. Barteau's command went after Hatch and caught up with the Second Iowa at Palo Alto where it had halted for lunch, eight miles from the road junction, and about five miles northwest of West Point. Barteau ordered a charge.

**APRIL 21
1863**

Clashes with Confederate cavalry at Palo Alto

**APRIL 21
1863**

Grierson pushes south through Starkville

Hatch deployed his men and gun. A short, sharp action ensued where the firepower of the repeating rifles stopped the charge. Then the lone Woodruff gun joined in. It was the first time many of the militia troops with Barteau had been under artillery fire. They scattered and ran. Hatch took this opportunity to remount his regiment and ride north to Okolona. Over the next two days Hatch's men rode north with Barteau following and increasing numbers of Confederate troops joining the pursuit. But the Second Iowa outran them all, burning bridges as they crossed, slowing the chase. In going through northern Mississippi swamps, they ran across slaves sent into the swamps with their masters' horses. Slaves and horses joined the Union cause, and by the time the Second Iowa safely reached La Grange its numbers had been swelled by 200 "contrabands" leading 600 spare horses.

Yet Hatch's biggest accomplishment was to give Grierson an open road south. The Second Iowa's repeating rifles convinced Ruggles that Barteau had caught a full cavalry brigade, not merely a regiment. While other

Colonel Edward Hatch commanded the Second Iowa during Grierson's Raid. He was one of the outstanding Union cavalry generals of the Civil War, and invited to take a Regular Army commission afterwards. This picture shows him as a young brigadier general during the Civil War. (LOC)

Confederate units reported contacts with Grierson on April 21, these were initially dismissed as diversions. Grierson pushed south, keeping to the road for speed until he reached Starkville, at 4:00 pm. There Grierson captured Confederate government mail and supplies, reading the mails and destroying the supplies. He continued south from Starkville, cutting through swamps, riding belly-deep in mud and water for five miles. It was fully dark before they found an island high enough to encamp for the night. They had traveled 25 miles under wretched conditions, and the miserable weather precluded any real chance for sleep that night, but they were now poised to accomplish their main objective.

Sixth Day – April 22

Grierson's predicament now was concealing his intentions while gaining information about his surroundings. He was deep within enemy territory, and completely on his own. That night he found a solution to these problems. The quartermaster sergeant of the Second Iowa, Richard Surby, volunteered to lead a squad of scouts. Surby proposed to Lieutenant Colonel Blackburn, the Seventh Illinois' executive officer, that Surby be allowed to recruit a dozen men willing to dress in civilian clothing, armed with weapons captured from the enemy. These scouts could pass themselves off as Confederates, allowing them to gain valuable intelligence.

The plan was risky. Any scout captured while dressed in this manner could be executed as a spy. In 1862 eight participants in the Andrews Raid – an attempt to steal a Confederate locomotive – were hanged after being captured because they were wearing civilian clothing when they stole the train. Abel Streight had asked his superiors for permission to dress scouts as Southern civilians before starting his raid, and had been forbidden from doing so. But Grierson did not know of the orders given to Streight. Blackburn forwarded Surby's suggestion and Grierson agreed to the plan.

Surby found eight volunteers, primarily among the Seventh Illinois. Their comrades held their carbines and uniforms and these scouts were soon ranging far outside Grierson's lines. The two regiments got into the spirit of the game, dubbing the squad the "Butternut Guerrillas" after the butternut-colored clothing worn in the South and by the squad. Confederates were not the only risk faced by these men. Coordinating their efforts with Grierson's pickets was critical, lest they get shot while attempting to return to friendly lines. Nevertheless, over the next week the Butternut Guerrillas gave Grierson a badly needed edge.

That night runaway slaves told Grierson about a Confederate leather factory near Starkville. Grierson dispatched a battalion of the Seventh Illinois, led by Major John Graham. They soon found the place, and captured it, along with a quartermaster officer from Port Hudson. The place was filled with boots, hats, saddles, and tack awaiting shipment to the Confederate army at Vicksburg. Graham had the buildings torched.

The battalion was back at the camp before dawn, and at sunrise the two regiments saddled up and continued to Louisville. The ride was through Noxubee River bottomlands, a maze of thickly wooded swamp. Much of

APRIL 22
1863

Starkville leather
factory burned

the 28-mile trip was made through mud and mire belly-deep for a horse. The artillery was broken down and packed across on horseback.

Before reaching Louisville, Grierson sent off two more diversions. He sent Captain Henry Forbes of the Seventh Illinois with his command, Company B, to Macon, Mississippi. Forbes was told to break the Gulf and Ohio railroad, cut the telegraph line at Macon, and then rejoin the column. He had only 32 men with which to accomplish this, but set forth with a will. Shortly after the company left, Grierson dispatched two more volunteers – Captain John Lynch and Corporal Jonathan Ballard of the Sixth Illinois – to cut the telegraph line that paralleled the railroad. These men rode in civilian disguise. He also sent a battalion of the Sixth Illinois ahead to Louisville, to take the town and keep inhabitants from leaving with word of Grierson's approach.

By this time Grierson was well ahead of news of his approach. Once the column was clear of the swamp, local civilians who spotted the force assumed it was Confederate. At one point, students at a school were turned out to cheer as "Van Dorn's cavalry" passed. At another spot Grierson requisitioned food from a mill. The owner grumbled about the slowness of receiving payment from the Confederate government, and told the Yanks that they should be chasing down Grierson instead of robbing him. The Yankees took care not to spoil the illusion. Shortly before reaching Louisville, they captured a Port Hudson-bound mail coach carrying government money and letters. Both were confiscated.

It was dusk by the time the column reached Louisville, but they pushed through the town without halting. Ten miles beyond the town Grierson found some high, dry ground at the Estes Plantation, and finally halted for the night. In all, the raiders had pushed over 50 miles deeper into Confederate territory that day. They were now only 40 miles from their objective – the Southern Railroad.

By now Pemberton knew there was a deep raid into his district, but did not know its objective. On one level, he knew that a raid in eastern Mississippi was an attempt to draw troops away from the Mississippi River. He would not fall into that trap – the garrisons at Grand Gulf and Vicksburg remained unchanged. However, he was forced to commit reserve troops – mainly those from Loring's division. Pemberton's assumption was that the Gulf and Ohio was its objective. He sent orders to Buford's brigade, dispersing the regiments along that rail line. He also sent General Loring from Camp Pemberton to Meridian, to coordinate activities in chasing down the Yankee cavalry. Pemberton's order cleared the Southern Railroad of Confederate troops from Jackson to Meridian.

Seventh Day – April 23

Grierson's men broke camp at daybreak, and continued south. The Woodruff guns were remounted. The carriage of one gun had broken, so it was mounted on buggy wheels, taken from the plantation. Grierson was nearing the Pearl River, the last terrain barrier before his objective. It was too deep to ford. To capture a bridge before it could be destroyed, Surby and his scouts

APRIL 23
1863

Philadelphia
captured

were sent ahead. There they found five civilians armed with shotguns preparing the bridge for destruction. Through a combination of bluff and threats, Surby convinced the men to run or surrender without fighting. Surby's men replaced the removed planks, allowing the bridge to be used.

The men demolishing the bridge were from Philadelphia, Mississippi, the brigade's next destination. The ones who escaped rode home, warning of the approaching column. Locals began sniping at the approaching scouts, and when Surby reached Philadelphia he found a crowd of armed militia blocking the road. Surby rode back to the advanced guard, and got ten troopers. With these men and his squad, he returned to Philadelphia, and charged into the armed mob. The militiamen scattered, and the Yanks captured six prisoners and nine horses. Among the prisoners was the county judge, who had organized the resistance.

By the time this brief battle was over, the rest of the brigade had reached and surrounded Philadelphia, preventing anyone from leaving. Grierson rode into town to sort things out. He was informed by the judge that he had gathered an armed party to keep the town from being looted and burned. Grierson gave an impromptu speech in the town square, stating that his men had strict orders to destroy only Confederate government property. No further resistance was offered, and Grierson's men finally rode out of Philadelphia at 3:00 pm, Grierson leaving a rear guard, commanded by Colonel Prince, to keep word of the Union presence from spreading. Prince lined up the town's inhabitants and had them swear to keep silent for the rest of the day.

As they were leaving for Decatur the column was overtaken by Lynch and Ballard, who reported that they had failed in their attempt to cut the telegraph line. The two had reached Macon at 8:00 am that day, where they were

William Surby and his "Butternut Guerrillas" were able to save the bridge over the Pearl River north of Philadelphia, Mississippi, through a combination of bluff and speed. Its capture enabled Grierson's men to reach Newton ahead of news of their arrival. (MOA)

APRIL 24 1863

Newton Station destroyed

stopped by the picket. The two Yankees spun a tale about being part of a militia unit at Enterprise, Mississippi, which had been visited by Yankee cavalry the day before. They explained to the picket that they had been sent to Macon with word of the raider. The two learned that Macon was occupied by three Confederate regiments including reinforcements from Mobile, Alabama.

Realizing they had no chance of cutting the telegraph, Lynch made an excuse to allow him to leave. Once out of sight, they rode hell for leather to catch up with their old command. Their most valuable contribution was to refocus attention on the Gulf and Ohio. Confederate reinforcements were sent to Enterprise instead of where they could have been useful.

Forbes and his company had likewise approached Macon on the previous evening. These men had looped north around the town and, doing some careful scouting, they captured a few straggling Confederates. Forbes similarly learned that Macon was too well garrisoned for a company – or even the whole brigade – to raid. They camped the night at a plantation three miles from Macon and on April 23 they gave up Macon as a bad job, and began riding back, seeking Grierson. En route they captured a Confederate soldier, and pressed him into service as a guide. The company was north of the Noxubee, which was unfordable, near Macon. They tried to ride over a bridge they had used previously, only to find that it was now guarded by a force too strong for a cavalry company to challenge. So they had to go upstream to find a place to cross. The delay left them more than a day behind Grierson.

Meanwhile, Grierson and the main body were pressing south. They camped at a plantation five to seven miles south of Philadelphia, but they rested there only until 10:00 pm. They were a long day's ride from the Southern Railroad but Grierson, with his innate feel for timing, felt the need

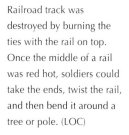

Railroad track was destroyed by burning the ties with the rail on top. Once the middle of a rail was red hot, soldiers could take the ends, twist the rail, and then bend it around a tree or pole. (LOC)

to press on. He sensed that the road ahead of him was open, and that while Newton was unguarded, it might not remain so for long.

Grierson was right: Forbes and his company had been spotted near Macon. Lynch had reported Union troops at Enterprise, and reports that Pemberton was receiving multiplied the size of the Union raid. The speed with which Grierson moved increased the confusion. Graham's raid on the leatherworks near Starkville occurred on April 22, but was not reported to Pemberton until April 25. This was leading Pemberton and his subordinates to cast about for Grierson well north of his actual position. Although reports were coming in from all over, the greatest number of sightings was being reported close to the Gulf and Ohio. Pemberton's attention was focused at the wrong point.

Eighth Day– April 24: Newton Station

After a short stop south of Philadelphia, Grierson was again on the march. The brief rest refreshed his men, and they rode through the rest of the night. Grierson sent an advance force ahead – two battalions of the Seventh Illinois, led by Lieutenant Colonel Blackburn. They were supposed to secure Decatur, Mississippi, the final town before Newton, and then scout Newton ahead of the rest of the brigade.

Blackburn, in turn, sent out Surby and his scouts to reconnoiter, who were again mistaken for Van Dorn's cavalry by the locals. Surby learned that the only Confederate troops in Newton were 150 convalescents in an army hospital there, but that large numbers of troops had moved through Newton heading east in the past few days.

Blackburn passed Decatur before sunrise, and then pressed on to Newton. He halted outside around 7:00 am, and sent Surby with two scouts to learn the situation. Surby wandered around the town, learning that there was a westbound freight train approaching Newton and that there was also a passenger train due at 9:00 am. By then it was around 8:00 am. Surby sent one scout back to Blackburn with news of the approaching trains.

Blackburn and his men rode in and took the town, capturing the hospital, before the freight train arrived. Pickets were sent to secure the town exits, while other men hid by the switches to the siding, and the rest of the troopers concealed themselves from the railroad. All this took place without a shot. The train – 25 cars long – puffed into the station and found itself trapped, shunted on to a siding. After taking the crew off, the Yankee cavalrymen hid. The eastbound train – a mixed passenger and freight – was also surprised and captured.

Blackburn and the Seventh Illinois set to work destroying both trains. The freight train was filled with ordinance and commissary stores bound for Vicksburg, as well as timbers and planking to repair railroad trestles. The eastbound train contained one passenger car of civilians fleeing Vicksburg. Two of the freight cars contained their goods. Of the rest, four contained ammunition and six commissary stores. The passengers' possessions were not military contraband, but the cars were. The troopers unloaded both baggage and furniture off the boxcars, the train's cars were moved to the sidetrack with the freight, and all of the cars torched.

There was a critical shortage of locomotives in the Confederacy. Most were the 4-4-0 "American" configuration, with four guide wheels and four drive wheels, like this destroyed Southern locomotive. (LOC)

By the time Grierson and the main body were in earshot, the ammunition in the burning boxcars had started exploding. Thinking the noise was the sound of battle, the main body came in a rush, to aid their comrades. When Grierson arrived, he was both annoyed at the scare and relieved there were no Confederate combatants in town, and set the brigade to work in earnest.

Grierson was aware that there were a lot of Confederates on the Gulf and Mobile. He dispatched two battalions of the Sixth Illinois under Major Starr with instructions to destroy bridges, trestles, and telegraph lines east of Newton. He sent Captain Hening and the third battalion of the Seventh Illinois west with similar instructions.

In Newton, the brigade had taken 75 prisoners from the hospital. These men were released on parole – they signed a statement pledging to take no further part in the war until properly exchanged for Union prisoners. This proved extremely popular as it effectively gave these men home leave until exchanged. A Confederate warehouse filled with clothing, weapons, coffee, and sugar had been found and was burned. But Grierson allowed the paroled prisoners to join his men in removing such of the clothing (which were captured Union uniforms) and consumables as they could use and carry off before burning the building.

In addition to the warehouse, the railroad depot and facilities were burned, telegraph equipment removed or destroyed, and the two locomotives exploded. Railroad ties were burned, and the fires used to heat the rails so that they could be bent and twisted. As previously, civilian buildings were spared. Soldiers even joined in with townspeople to douse fires in houses accidentally started by exploding ammunition.

By 2:00 pm the work of destruction was complete. Major Matthew Starr, of the Sixth Illinois, returned with a report that three bridges and several hundred feet of trestle and track had been destroyed over an eight-mile stretch east of Newton, along with telegraph lines and poles. This included the bridge over the Chunky River. Hening's force had similarly torn down telegraph lines and burned a bridge half a mile west of Newton. The brigade mounted up and headed south.

Having achieved his primary mission, Grierson's objective was now survival and escape. Since Grierson knew Confederate forces were seeking him north of Newton, he decided that safety lay to the South. To outrun pursuit and allow his men to recuperate he wanted to press on for another 15 to 20 miles.

At first their ride was slowed by refugees fleeing Newton. Once they learned that Grierson's brigade was leaving civilians and their property alone – Grierson even provided escorts back to Newton for those who wished to return – the flood became a trickle, opening the road. The citizens of Garlandville, two miles south of Newton, attempted to stop the raiders, turning out a militia primarily consisting of superannuated warriors armed with shotguns. A cavalry charge scattered them. Grierson confiscated their weapons and released them. One militiaman offered to serve as a guide, revealing pro-Union sentiments once out of town. The brigade rode another 12 miles before camping for the night at the Bender Plantation, two miles west of Montrose, Mississippi.

In the meantime Forbes and his company rode south in pursuit of Grierson. By noon they had reached Philadelphia only to learn that Grierson was long gone. They pressed south, but their progress was slowed by snipers and guerrillas – the country had been stirred up by Grierson's passage. By nightfall they passed through Decatur, and camped two miles south of that town. The next day, they told themselves, they would catch up with Grierson at Newton.

The Confederates were also searching for Grierson but looking in the wrong place, still focused on defending the Gulf and Ohio Railroad. April 24 passed with a frustrating lack of intelligence. The only clue that something had happened was a negative one – a lack of telegraph traffic through Newton. Messengers from Newton were carrying word, but they were riding exhausted horses left behind by Grierson, who confiscated all good horses he found as remounts.

Ninth Day – April 25

April 25 was a Saturday, but Grierson intended it as a day of rest. He allowed his men, who had had four hours' sleep between the dawn of April 23 and sunset on April 24, to sleep until sunrise. The next few hours were spent tending to gear and horses, eating a leisurely meal (unwillingly provided by their host), and planning. They did recompense the plantation's owner by providing a receipt for goods confiscated. Of course, the receipt was worthless until the Yankees occupied that part of Mississippi.

ENTERPRISE

APRIL 25, 1863

Captain Henry Forbes brought Company B of the Seventh Illinois to Enterprise in search of Grierson's brigade, which he had been told was heading there. Unfortunately, this was disinformation planted by Grierson to confuse any pursuers. Instead, Forbes found a Confederate infantry regiment entrenched in the town, with a second regiment unloading by rail car. Rather than surrender or fight against suicidal odds, Forbes called for a parley and demanded the surrender of Enterprise in the name of Benjamin Grierson. While the garrison discussed the possibility of surrender, Forbes and his men took the opportunity to escape to the west.

UNION FORCES

1 Company B, Seventh Illinois, commanded by Captain Henry Forbes
2 Captain Henry Forbes and Union delegation

CONFEDERATE FORCES

1 35th Alabama Infantry, commanded by Colonel Edwin Goodwin
2 Confederate infantry regiment arriving by train
3 Colonel Edwin Goodwin and Confederate delegation

Grierson knew that the Gulf and Ohio was heavily garrisoned. Although he had left hints that he was headed that way to occupants of the towns through which he had passed, he had no intention of heading east. He also felt that it would be unwise to retrace his path. He planned to ride east for a day or two, and collect reports from his scouts. He then planned to cut north, crossing the Southern between Jackson and Lake, and then ride through central Mississippi. Alternatively, Grant was due to land at Grand Gulf. If the way north was blocked, Grierson could continue east and link up with Grant.

Regardless, the horses were in poor shape after all the hard riding. Grierson confiscated the stock he found at Bender's Plantation. He also planned an easy ride west. Accompanied by two slaves – the first of many that Grierson would accumulate over the last half of his travels – the brigade started off at 8:00 am.

They traveled only five miles before resting at another plantation, where the only occupants were five women, at least one of whom was pro-Union. While most of the brigade rested until 2:00 pm, Grierson dispatched parties to find horses hidden in the swamps, woods, or byroads. Afterwards they continued their westward progress, finally stopping when night fell at the Mackadora Plantation 17 miles west of their starting point.

From there Grierson began another diversion. He chose Sam Nelson, one of Surby's Butternut Guerrillas, for a single-handed raid on the telegraph line that paralleled the Southern Railroad. If possible, Nelson was to fire a bridge or trestle. The man left at midnight.

Meanwhile, Forbes' company continued their pursuit of their brigade. They galloped to Newton, where they found that Grierson had been and gone. Grierson's generosity towards civilians and combatants paid dividends at this point, because the townspeople and paroled prisoners gave the Yankees a cordial greeting, politely answering Forbes' questions. Forbes learned of the fight at Garlandville, and that Grierson had indicated he was heading east toward the Gulf, and Mobile afterwards. There were also rumors of Yankees at Enterprise, Mississippi, garbled retellings of the sighting of Forbes and his men at Macon.

So off the company went to Enterprise, and through hard riding arrived a little after 1:00 pm. The intelligence they gathered en route indicated that there were no Confederate troops there, so they rode within sight of the town. To their dismay they saw a regiment of Confederate infantry in Enterprise, and another regiment unloading from a newly arrived train. It was too large a force to fight, and they were too close to escape. Surrender was undesirable.

Forbes decided upon a bold course. He approached the town with a small party under a flag of truce. While panicky Confederate sentries fired shots at the approaching men, Forbes persisted, riding up to a barricade, and demanding to speak to the commanding officer. He was met by Colonel Edwin Goodwin, commanding the 35th Alabama Infantry, garrisoning Enterprise.

Forbes then demanded the surrender of the garrison. He informed Goodwin that Brigadier General Benjamin Grierson (giving Grierson an unofficial promotion) had a brigade of cavalry poised to attack the town, but wished to offer an opportunity to surrender to spare bloodshed. Goodwin asked for an hour in which to consider a response, and Forbes replied that he had the authority to grant the request. The parley ended with Forbes stating that he would be back in an hour for the answer, and both groups departed.

The Confederates spent the hour further fortifying their position – sending to Macon for further reinforcements, forwarding the note given to them by Forbes. Forbes and his men used the time to flee to the west. No second parley was held. Once safely away, the company decided to continue after Grierson, so they retraced their path, reaching Garlandville by dusk. There Forbes found that the Garlandville militia had reconstituted itself into a 60-man force of "Garlandville Avengers." One of Forbes' scouts, in butternut disguise, convinced the Avengers' picket that Forbes' men were Alabama cavalry seeking Grierson. The Yankees passed through the town unmolested. The Garlandville men even provided the scouts with information on Grierson's previous appearances and probable destination. They rode west until well past midnight, stopping at Hodge's Plantation for a few hours' sleep.

For the Confederate command, April 25 was the day the thunderbolt fell. Word finally reached both Pemberton in Vicksburg and Loring in Meridian of the previous day's destruction of Newton Station. Other reports trickled in to Pemberton throughout the day – word that a leatherworks at Starkville had been burned, and that Yankee cavalry brigades had been seen at Enterprise and Macon. As a result, Pemberton's focus changed from Grant's movements on the river to Grierson's raid. No one had dreamed that the Yankees would penetrate to the Southern Railroad, and Pemberton suddenly realized how vulnerable Vicksburg would be if that supply line were permanently cut.

Grierson's extraordinary mobility was achieved through a willingness to travel through seemingly impassible terrain. More than once his column rode for hours with the horses belly-deep in water and mud. (AC)

A flurry of orders went out. Pemberton sent General Adams and his force from Jackson to Lake, just west of Newton. He ordered troops from Fort Pemberton to cover the Southern from Morton, Mississippi, to Jackson. He sent artillery to the Big Black Bridge to cover the railroad crossing there. He ordered the cavalry under Wirt Adams to search for Grierson. He also sent messages to the Grand Gulf and Port Hudson garrisons to be on the lookout for the Yankee cavalry, and to send what cavalry they had in search of the raiders.

Word was passed to Ruggles that Barteau and his cavalry had been deceived by a decoy force. The exhausted Confederate cavalry again cast south, determined to keep Grierson from escaping once more if he came north. Loring moved his forces up and down the Gulf and Ohio, and west along the Southern Railroad to the Chunky River. Grierson's men had successfully hit Newton, but the Confederates wanted to extract a price for that success.

Tenth Day – April 26

The ferry over the Pearl River was captured when the ferryman mistook a Union scout for a Confederate cavalryman. Capture of the ferry intact allowed the brigade to cross the Pearl River 24 men and horses at a time. (MOA)

Grierson's day started early. Nelson returned before dawn with an alarming report: he had not reached the Southern, having been stopped by Confederate cavalry. Nelson had convinced their commander that he was a paroled Confederate. He also decoyed the Confederates by reporting that Grierson had been in Garlandville with 1,800 men the previous day at noon, and that they were heading east toward the Gulf and Ohio. Nelson hurried back to Grierson after giving the Confederates directions to Garlandville. The cavalry force was large enough to challenge Grierson, and they would soon find the tracks left by the Yankees the previous day.

Other scouts reported that all of the Southern Railroad stations between Jackson and Lake were garrisoned, and that Grant was soon expected to attempt a landing at Grand Gulf. Breaking camp at 6:00 am, Grierson decided to push west and link up with Grant. They passed around Pineville, across the Leaf River, through Raleigh, and on through Westville after dark. Along the way they were joined by a number of slaves – free and runaway – who delighted in showing the Yankees where "master" was hiding his food and horses. The cavalrymen burned the bridge at Leaf River to slow pursuit, and captured the sheriff of Smith County at Raleigh, relieving him of $3,000 in Confederate government money. They spent the night at the Williams Plantation two miles west of Westville. The owner, in residence, was a Confederate officer on leave. He was captured and paroled.

Forbes and his party resumed their pursuit of Grierson. They too pushed west shortly after dawn, and were soon on the track of their brigade. Unfortunately, they were slowed when they reached each stream or river by the bridges burned by their comrades. They took time to cast for fords, swimming their horses across at some points. Then, at Raleigh as at Garlandville, they discovered a militia had formed to protect the town. This time B Company dispensed with trickery. Charging the militiamen, B Company scattered them, winning through the town.

Forbes asked for three volunteers to press on ahead of the company. His brother, Sergeant Stephen Forbes, and two privates stripped their horses of all unessential equipment – including their carbines and sabers – and pushed them down the road as fast as possible. The three would ride all night, followed by the rest of the company.

Forbes' company was lucky to have avoided the cavalry Nelson had encountered. These troops had hared off to Garlandville, and so were out of the chase. Pemberton was receiving a flurry of reports of Union cavalrymen throughout Mississippi, and phantom Yankees were again spotted near Enterprise. There was even a report of 1,000 Northern cavalry at Kosciusko, well north of the Southern Railroad, but threatening the Mississippi Central line. The most accurate report came from General John Adams, who stated that Grierson and 800 Yankee cavalry were 15 miles south of Lake, and would probably attack either Forrest or Lake. But this report was ignored.

Instead, Pemberton sent a brigade to cover the Mississippi Central line, and focused attention on the Gulf and Ohio. Pemberton also directed Wirt Adams and his cavalry to cover Claiborne and Jefferson Counties, to catch Grierson if Grierson was headed to the Mississippi. He also sent an urgent telegram to his superior, General Joseph Johnston, requesting the immediate return of Van Dorn's cavalry. Unfortunately, these men were either raiding northern Tennessee or chasing Abel Streight through Alabama and Georgia.

Eleventh Day – April 27: Hazelhurst

Grierson made an early start Monday morning, sending Prince and two battalions of the Seventh Illinois off well before daybreak. They were to push on to the Pearl River, and secure a ferry across the river. Grierson

APRIL 25 1863

Confederate command learns of the attacks on Starkville and Newton Station

APRIL 27 1863

Hazelhurst Station destroyed

had learned of the ferry from the captured sheriff – it offered one of the few ways across the Pearl, which was too deep to ford and too wide to swim south of Jackson.

Prince reached the ferry before dawn through hard marching, and captured it intact, when the ferryman brought it to the east bank, thinking that the Seventh Illinois were Confederate cavalry. Prince immediately sent a party across to hold the far bank, and waited for the rest of the brigade. Grierson started the rest of his force two hours after Prince, and was close behind. They were crossing the Strong River and making preparations to burn the bridge when Sergeant Forbes and his party came riding up, reporting that the rest of Forbes' company was behind them. Grierson strengthened the party at the bridge to serve as a rear guard, to hold it until Forbes' Company B rejoined the brigade. Once Captain Forbes and his company crossed the bridge, Sergeant Forbes set fire to it.

Meanwhile, at the Pearl River the brigade was slowly crossing, 24 horses at a time. Prince sent two scouts, dressed in butternut, ahead to Hazelhurst, the next town, and a depot for the New Orleans, Jackson and Great Northern Railroad (NOJ&GN). The two scouts boldly rode into town with a message to be telegraphed to Pemberton. It reported the ferry had been destroyed and the Yankees were trapped east of the Pearl River. They cut the telegraph after leaving the town, preventing any amendment of that report.

The NOJ&GN was part of the main supply line for Grand Gulf. While neither Hazelhurst nor the NOJ&GN were part of the original plan for the raid, Grierson was in a position to attack it as he had hammered Newton. Grierson and Prince were not going to let that opportunity slip. Prince swept in with the advance guard in the late morning, capturing a string of boxcars loaded with munitions – mainly heavy shells. As at Newton, they heard that a second train was due, so they prepared an ambush. Unfortunately for the Yankees, the engineer sensed something wrong as he approached the station. Abruptly he stopped the train and threw the engine into reverse, backing out of danger faster than the cavalrymen could pursue.

A thunderstorm that had been threatening then opened up; Hazelhurst was experiencing a torrential downpour. This slowed, but did not stop, the destruction of track, both ties and rails. The town was searched, but no weapons were discovered in private homes. A cache of food for the Confederate army was found, and taken to a hotel to be cooked up for the brigade. Prince pushed the boxcars down the tracks, and burned those. Unfortunately, the filled shells exploded with enough force to set several homes on fire, despite the rain. As at Newton, Grierson and the main body heard the explosions and came at a charge, assuming that Prince's force was being attacked. Instead the only enemy they found was fire, which they helped the townspeople to fight.

At 6:00 pm the brigade mounted up and headed west to Gallatin, and southwest afterward. Shortly after passing Gallatin they stumbled on a Confederate 64-pound Parrott, which was being pulled to Grand Gulf. The carriage and ammunition wagons were burned, and the gun spiked.

Throughout, it was raining heavily. Grierson and his men finally camped for the night, four miles southwest of Gallatin at Thompson's Plantation.

For Pemberton, April 27 must have seemed like the continuation of a waking nightmare. In the morning he received reports of Yankees near the Pearl River. Pemberton sent a warning to Bowen at Grand Gulf that Grierson might be headed his way and to be alert. Orders were sent to destroy the ferry over the Pearl River, orders apparently carried out, based on telegraphic reports from Hazelhurst that arrived with a promptness that would have been admirable had it not been the message Sergeant Surby had hoaxed the telegraph into sending. Soon afterward Pemberton received a telegraph from Crystal Springs – where the train that escaped at Hazelhurst had gone – that Hazelhurst was in Union hands. Alarmed, Pemberton ordered reinforcements to Big Black Bridge. If that were burned, Vicksburg would be untenable. He also ordered Barteau's cavalry from northeast Mississippi to Hazelhurst, and ordered Gardner at Port Hudson to intercept Grierson.

Gardner responded by sending the Ninth Tennessee Cavalry to Clinton and Woodville. One company went up the NOJ&GN line to Jackson, and then Clinton, while the rest of the regiment hurried to Woodville, to head to Clinton from there. Both groups were following a path east of Grierson's location and intended direction.

Grierson's Raid inspired hundreds of black slaves to run away and seek freedom with the Yankee forces. Nearly 1,200 former slaves crossed into Union lines with either Grierson's or Hatch's columns. (LOC)

HAZELHURST

APRIL 27, 1863

At Hazelhurst, Lieutenant Colonel Blackburn hoped to repeat his successful ambush of an arriving train. However, the troopers of the Seventh Illinois were careless, and the train's engineer was more alert than at Newton. Sensing a trap, the engineer stopped his train, then reversed it, driving north to safety before the Union cavalrymen could catch it. Grierson and his men had to settle for destroying the rolling stock actually in the town and depot. Unfortunately, they underestimated the ferocity of the burning ammunition in the parked boxcars. The explosion set fire to several homes, and Grierson's men joined forces with the townspeople to put them out.

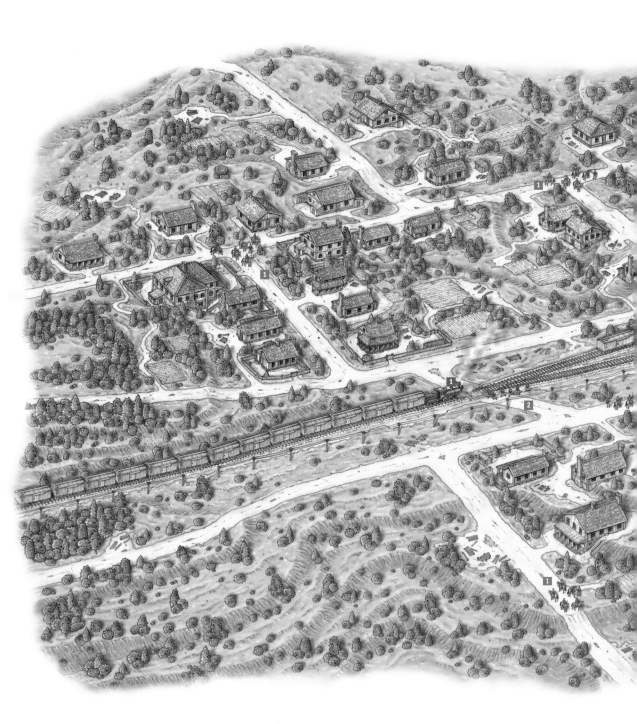

UNION FORCES

1 Union cavalrymen posted around the town to prevent word of the town's capture reaching Confederate forces

2 Union cavalrymen attempting to capture the Confederate train

CONFEDERATE FORCES

1 Confederate train

▼ EVENTS

1 Rolling stock burning

2 Buildings set on fire by the burning ammunition.

3 Grierson accepting the paroles of captured Confederate soldiers

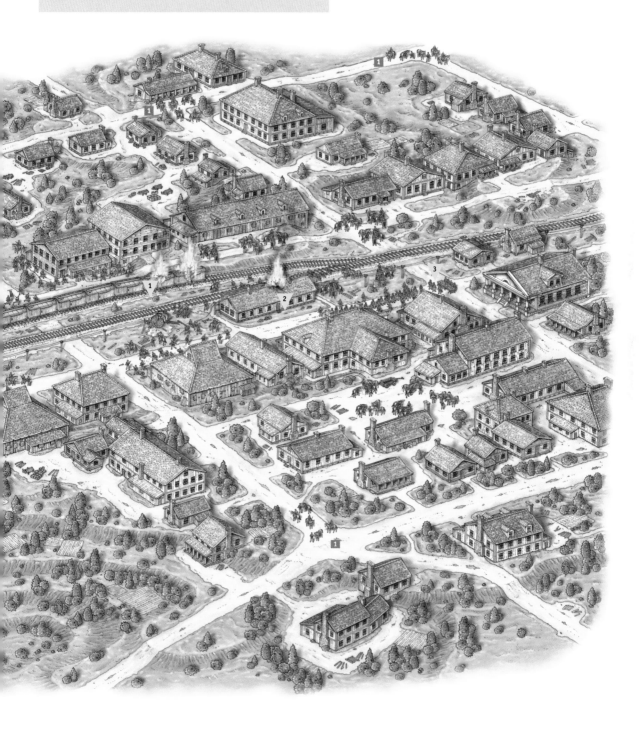

Pemberton received one good piece of news that day. Loring reported that there were no Union cavalry near Enterprise, and that the previous reports exaggerated the size of Yankee forces threatening the Gulf and Ohio. Loring also suggested that Grierson was probably heading toward Baton Rouge – an appraisal that would have been useful days earlier, but was now too old to be worthwhile.

Twelfth Day – April 28

Grierson's raiders made an early start on April 28, hitting the road at 6:00 am. Grierson knew that he was far too close to large Confederate troop concentrations for comfort, and was determined to push on and join Grant at Grand Gulf. After traveling a little way west, Grierson launched yet another diversion. This time he sent a battalion of the Seventh Illinois – Companies A, H, F, and M – under the command of Captain George W. Trafton to strike the New Orleans railroad south of Hazlehurst, at Byhalia. The rest of the command rode west, toward Union Church.

When stopped for lunch at Snyder's Plantation, two miles northwest of town, the pickets were fired upon by a group of mounted men. These proved to be advanced elements of Wirt Adams' cavalry, searching for Grierson. The exchange grew into a running skirmish, as the Yankees counterattacked and then pushed the Confederate cavalry back through Union Church. The Yanks held the town and bivouacked the night there.

Meanwhile, Trafton and his force reached Byhalia, and found it undefended. There was a Confederate camp there, but Trafton arrived while the troops were out hunting Yankees. Instead, the Yanks destroyed the camp and a burned a store of coal there. They then swept into Byhalia, destroyed the depot building, commissary stores, the water tower, a long railroad trestle near the depot, and a stationary steam engine that powered a water pump and sawmill. They also captured a Confederate quartermaster corps major.

On the way back to Grierson – who told them to rendezvous at Union Church – the scouts learned of the presence of Wirt Adams' cavalry in the area, including a rough estimate of their strength – about 500 troopers and six artillery pieces. Better still they learned that Wirt Adams had set up an ambush on the trail between Union Church and Fayette, Mississippi – the route that Grierson had planned to take the next day. They told Grierson of the planned ambush when they arrived at the brigade's bivouac at 3:00 am on April 29.

On April 28 Pemberton was redoubling his efforts to trap Grierson. He moved troops to Hazlehurst and Brookhaven to protect the New Orleans Railroad, and sent both an infantry and a cavalry regiment to Woodville to cut off any attempt to double back. Reports drifting in indicated that Grierson was going west, not south, so Pemberton sent a wire to Adams, advising the colonel that Grierson might be headed his way. Adams sent a patrol of 100 men to Union Church to scout. They soon made contact, but realized they were badly outnumbered. Their commander, Stephen Cleaveland, sent word to Adams, who moved to Union Church. While Adams had artillery, his force was outnumbered two to one. Adams decided he could not attack Grierson, so he set up the ambush on the road to Fayette.

Pemberton also cautioned Bowen at Grand Gulf to watch out for Grierson. Bowen had bigger worries than Grierson, however; he saw that Grant was loading troops up at Hard Times, Louisiana, for Grant's push across the river.

Thirteenth Day – April 29

When Trafton arrived with word of Adams at 3:00 am, Grierson was woken and given the news. From intelligence gathered through his scouts and provided by local blacks, eager to help the Yankees, Grierson learned that he had arrived at the vicinity of Grand Gulf too soon. Grant had not yet landed. Grierson was also aware that waiting for Grant would be suicidal. Forting up would only allow Pemberton to concentrate on Grierson.

Grierson decided to head for Baton Rouge, but also decided to convince his opposition that he was going in a different direction. The twenty-one

Wirt Adams led the Confederate cavalry that remained in western Mississippi after Van Dorn and most of the rest of Pemberton's cavalry were transferred to Tennessee. Adams almost caught Grierson, to be foiled by Grierson's unrelenting pace. (AC)

APRIL 28 1863

Confederate camp at Byhalia destroyed

APRIL 29 1863

Brookhaven captured

APRIL 30 1863

Bogue Chitto and Summit depots destroyed

prisoners taken the previous day were paroled, after hearing Grierson and his officers discuss the best way to Grand Gulf and Natchez. To cap this, Grierson allowed a civilian prisoner to overhear plans to ride to Natchez, and then allowed this man to "escape," unparoled.

Grierson then had a battalion of the Sixth Illinois create a diversion to the west, while the rest of the brigade slipped off to the east. The Sixth Illinois troops soon rejoined them after driving the screening Confederates back toward Wirt Adams' ambush. While the Confederates hid, waiting silently for the Yanks to spring the trap, Grierson's men plunged into thickets east of Union Church. Over the next few hours, in Sergeant Surby's words, "I do not think we missed traveling towards any point on the compass. The dodging succeeded in its goal of losing Adams. Adams did not discover that Grierson was elsewhere until 2:00 pm when a patrol sent to Union Church discovered it was deserted."

By then Grierson's men were approaching Brookhaven. Shortly after reaching the main road to the town they overran an ox and mule train carrying sugar. What sugar was not appropriated by Union troopers was destroyed. A scout of Brookhaven revealed several hundred Confederates in the town. Many did not have uniforms and few had arms ready, so Grierson felt that they would scatter if pressed. His assessment proved correct. The Confederate force, a mixture of recruits and militia, offered little resistance when the Seventh Illinois swept into town and over 200 were taken captive. Unwilling to carry so many prisoners, Grierson paroled them. Writing out the paroles took the adjutants the rest of the day – a process that lengthened as word went out that prisoners were being paroled. Many of the Confederates who had escaped returned to surrender, so that they too could sit out the war until exchanged. The rest of the brigade spent their time destroying the depot and railroad tracks. The Yanks made further friends by paying for all meals – with captured Confederate money. Finally they rode out of town, heading south for eight miles before stopping for the night well after dark.

Wirt Adams was not the only Confederate commander questing after Grierson's men that day. The previous day Pemberton had mounted the Twentieth Mississippi Infantry, then at Jackson, with the intention of having them pursue the raiders. He handed command of this force to Colonel Robert Richardson and gave Richardson orders to get Grierson. Unfortunately, Richardson could not get the force under way until the morning of April 29, assembling the force at the depot at 2:30 am. Departure was further delayed because the locomotive proved incapable of pulling the assembled cars, nor was there wood to fuel the engine. It was not until daybreak – after uncoupling several cars and crowding troops and horses in the remaining ones – that the train puffed out of Jackson.

It arrived at Hazelhurst around lunchtime. There townspeople claimed that Grierson was returning, so the unit scouted the immediate area for non-existent Yankees. Finally reports drifted in that Grierson was in Union Church, so the mounted infantry went off that way. When they arrived at 9:00 pm they learned from some of Adam's men that Grierson had departed half a day earlier. Richardson rested two hours, and then headed back to Hazelhurst.

Fourteenth Day – April 30

When Grierson and his men started riding early on the morning of April 30, much was happening elsewhere that would affect his raid. Four groups of Confederate troops were converging on Grierson – Wirt Adams riding down to Osyka from Union Church, Richardson and his men following the railroad south from Hazelhurst, and the Ninth Tennessee Cavalry scouting southwest from Woodville. More ominously, Gardner at Port Hudson dispatched Miles' Legion – 2,400 troops including 300 cavalry and a number of guns – to cut off Grierson from Baton Rouge. Most were being sent to guard the crossings of the Amite River, which Grierson had to pass to reach Baton Rouge. Another force was sent to Osyka, to guard the supplies cached there.

Yet Grierson had not been forgotten by the Union Army. Sooy Smith finally learned from a spy that Grierson had struck Newton on April 24, and that Grierson was headed back north, through central Mississippi. The news was old and inaccurate, but Smith could not know that. To assist Grierson, Smith launched a number of raids into northern Mississippi. This included one commanded by Colonel Hatch, who had been given a three-regiment cavalry brigade that included his Second Iowa. Down the Mississippi, Grant, stymied at Grand Gulf the day before, shifted south and crossed the Mississippi River at Bruinsburg. He was marching on Port Gibson, which he would take the next day. Grant would learn of Grierson's activities when he read a Confederate newspaper in Port Gibson. It was the first indication Grant had of Grierson's presence since Hatch parted company

**MAY 1
1863**

**Skirmish at
Wall's Bridge**

At Summit, the Sixth and Seventh Illinois tore up track, and burned the depot, water tower, and 25 railroad cars. (MOA)

with Grierson. Grant's movement absorbed the attentions of both Bowen at Grand Gulf and Pemberton. Pemberton was too busy fighting Grant to further manage the pursuit, or to send additional troops after Grierson.

Grierson and his men plunged south without knowledge of any of this, however. On April 30 they followed the railroad, reaching Summit by noon, but the quick progress did not reduce the damage done to the railroad. From Gills Plantation to Summit the raiders burned every bridge, trestle, and water tower on the line. At Bogue Chitto they burned the depot, its contents, and 15 railroad cars. At Summit they destroyed twenty-five more railroad cars, a large quantity of Confederate government sugar, and the depot building. The line was so thoroughly wrecked that it could not be used again until after the war ended.

Grierson's men also found a large quantity of rum buried under a boardwalk. Fortunately Grierson learned of the cache before the men could liberate any significant quantity of the high-proof liquor. The barrels were smashed, rum watering the street. Grierson also discovered a significant amount of pro-Union sentiment in Summit among both its white and black inhabitants. Leaving Summit, Grierson struck off southwest, abandoning the railroad. The brigade rode another 15 miles before stopping for the night at the Spurlack Plantation, near Liberty, Mississippi.

Grierson's move away from the railroad proved prescient. Richardson made slow progress – mainly due to the destruction of the railroad wrought by Grierson's men – but reached the vicinity of Summit by midnight. Believing Grierson was encamped in Summit for the night, he prepared to launch an ambush at 3:00 am – to catch the Yankees sleeping. All Richardson's attack did was disturb the townspeople's sleep.

Adams had also moved south quickly. By nightfall he was within ten miles of Spurlack's plantation. To further complicate Grierson's escape, the Ninth Tennessee, hot on Grierson's trail, had arrived in Osyka.

Fifteenth Day – May 1

As dawn broke on May 1, two obstacles stood between Grierson's cavalry and safety – the Tickfaw and Amite Rivers. Grierson feared that the Confederate net was drawing tight around him. His scouts had provided reports of the converging Confederate columns and he resolved to ride hard for a bridge across the Tickfaw, but felt the need to further confuse the Confederates as to his intentions. As on previous days, he sent off small parties to make demonstrations towards Magnolia and Osyka – to again focus Confederate attention on the railroad.

Shortly after starting, the main column came across an old civilian heading for a mill. The travel-stained clothing worn by the Yankees was unrecognizable, and the man took the troopers for a Confederate unit seeking Grierson. Without correcting the man's mistake Grierson hired him as a guide. It was a worthwhile expenditure of Confederate money and a captured horse, because the old man knew the countryside intimately, and the column made fast progress. However, as they neared the bridge over the Tickfaw they saw fresh and numerous horse tracks on the road to Osyka.

Realizing this indicated that a significant enemy force was in the area, Grierson halted the column and sent scouts – dressed in Confederate butternut, as usual – to reconnoiter.

The scouts encountered a patrol of the Ninth Tennessee heading toward the bridge. While they were talking to the patrol, some other Confederate soldiers, straggling, blundered into some troopers of the Seventh Illinois and realized they were Yanks. A brief exchange took place, with the stragglers quickly captured. When the Confederate patrol investigated, they were told that it was an accidental exchange between two friendly units, and then were captured when they lowered their guard.

However, the exchange was also heard by Grierson's advance guard, led by Lieutenant Colonel Blackburn, approaching Wall's Bridge across the Tickfaw. Blackburn assumed the firing meant that their presence had become known to the Confederates, and charged across the bridge, calling the scouts – all he had with him – to join the charge. Blackburn's action proved ill advised. The scouts by themselves – dressed in butternut outfits – could likely have taken the bridge by bluff and surprise. The presence of a Union officer – in a Union officer's uniform – rushing the bridge gave the game away.

The defenders opened fire. Within a few minutes a firefight developed that left Blackburn fatally injured and two of the scouts, including Surby, badly wounded. Worse still, Blackburn and the scouts – injured and otherwise – were pinned down under enemy fire. The rest of the advance guard, one company of cavalry, rushed up to rescue their comrades, and the skirmish grew.

The bridge was held by three companies of the Ninth Louisiana Partisan Battalion – part of the force sent north with the Ninth Tennessee Cavalry to Woodville by Garner. They had gone on ahead to secure the bridge and soon pinned down the advance guard. Grierson and Prince heard the firing. Grierson sent a battalion of the Seventh Illinois to the bridge, and split the Sixth Illinois, sending half to ford the river on both flanks.

The superior numbers of the Seventh failed to force the bridge, but Grierson sent two of the Woodruff guns to support the attack. They soon deployed and began shelling the Partisan Ranger cavalry. The Louisiana irregulars reacted much as the Mississippi state forces had when Hatch's Woodruff gun opened up. They broke and ran. Once started, they did not stop until reaching Osyka.

While bloody, the fight was short, so short that Grierson's civilian guide failed to realize what had happened. He congratulated Grierson on driving off the Yankees, took his horse and cash, and returned to his original task. The fight left one of Grierson's men dying and three, including Sergeant Surby, too badly injured to travel. Grierson was forced to leave them at a plantation, along with his surgeon and a trooper who volunteered to remain. Surby's companions changed him back into a Union uniform, and one took the diary Surby had made of the raid. One of the wounded men later died. Surby, the doctor, and other two troopers were taken prisoner. Yet despite the cost, the way to Baton Rouge was now open – if only briefly. Gardner's troops were rushing to block passage over the Amite, and Adams and

OVERLEAF
When Lieutenant Colonel Blackburn learned that Confederate pickets were guarding the bridge over the Tickfaw River, he rashly charged across, supported by only a few scouts. The Confederates waited until the force was across the bridge before opening fire, mortally wounding Blackburn and one other scout, and injuring two others. The attack force was pinned down by enemy fire, and a general engagement developed in an effort to rescue the trapped men. It required artillery support from the Woodruff guns to end the stalemate that developed.

The federal cavalry camp where Grierson's men stayed after their arrival at Baton Rouge. (AC)

Richardson were in hot pursuit. They had joined forces in early afternoon at Magnolia, Mississippi, where both had gone seeking Grierson. By 10:00 pm they were at Osyka, and they headed south until 2:00 am, when they finally paused to rest.

Grierson made his first contact with Gardner's forces when the brigade encountered three companies of scouting cavalry near Greensburg at 2:00 pm. The Sixth Illinois drove them off, and Grierson broke contact. He reached William's Bridge across the Amite at midnight – ahead of Gardner's men – and was soon across the unfordable river.

Sixteenth Day – May 2

But Grierson sensed that it was no time to stop. The troopers rode doggedly toward Baton Rouge all night. By dawn they were at Greenwell Springs, where they found the camp of one of the Confederate cavalry units hunting them. Led by the Sixth Illinois, the brigade forded Sandy Creek and captured the camp, taking 40 prisoners. They destroyed the camp – 150 tents, ammunition, stores, and guns – before resuming the march.

There was one final river between Grierson and Baton Rouge – the Comite. It could be forded, but the three fords were guarded by Bryan's cavalry – a company that was part of Miles' Legion. Pickets were at two of the fords, with the bulk of the company and its camp at Robert's Ford. Because of the Comite's proximity to Baton Rouge, the Confederates' attentions were focused in that direction – to the south and west – rather than the bank from which Grierson's men were approaching. Led by the Seventh Illinois, the Union cavalry swept across the ford and captured the Confederate camp and company. Surprise was so total that only one man – an officer who hid in the branches of a moss-covered oak – escaped the Yankees.

At about the same time, Richardson and Adams were arriving at Greensburg. Richardson had sent a company of cavalry ahead to block Grierson by burning Williams' Bridge, but that force arrived eight hours too late. While digesting this intelligence at Newman's Plantation they were joined by Miles' Legion, also seeking the elusive Yankees. Grierson had slipped between both groups. Adams and Richardson were soon to rejoin Pemberton, to aid the fight against Grant, at Port Hudson. Colonel Miles received orders to cover the railroad, too late for it to do any good.

Grierson, his men, their prisoners – a swarm of runaway slaves that had been attaching themselves to the marauding Yankees since Montrose, Mississippi – and extra mules, horses, and wagons accumulated en route were past the last Confederate outpost between them and Baton Rouge. Everyone was exhausted. They had ridden 76 miles without sleep since rising at daybreak on April 30, fighting four battles in the intervening hours. Rather than risking friendly fire entering Baton Rouge, Grierson halted his men at a large plantation four miles past the Comite, intending to rest and send scouts to Baton Rouge. As related in the introduction, a sleeping orderly rode into the Union lines, and General Auger, commanding Baton Rouge, sent a patrol out to investigate. Grierson and his brigade received a heroes' welcome in Baton Rouge. It was not until 3:00 pm, following a victory parade, that the raiders received the thing they most wanted – an opportunity to have a full and uninterrupted night's sleep. Grierson's Raid was over.

ANALYSIS

MAY 2 1863

Grierson's force arrives at Baton Rouge

Grierson's Raid, in material terms, was possibly the most successful Union cavalry raid of the Civil War. In their wake the raiders destroyed much of value to the Confederate military – a leather factory, numerous warehouses loaded with food, munitions, and supplies needed by a materiel-starved army, and at least six different encampments, with associated tents and equipment. While these may seem trivial to modern readers, the South was hard pressed to feed, clothe, house, arm, and equip the soldier in its armies.

There were never enough shoes and boots to go round. Just the rumor of a warehouse filled with shoes was enough to draw Lee's army to Gettysburg, for example. Similarly, harness tack was always at a premium; bareback cavalry are not efficient warriors. Sleeping under the stars holds attractions – if done for a few nights in fine weather – but it quickly becomes miserable when cold or rainy and the Confederacy lacked replacements for the tents and camp equipment burned by Grierson.

More importantly, the raiders – in Sergeant Surby's words – "played smash with the railroads." Rails, rolling stock, and locomotives were irreplaceable in the Confederacy by 1863. The only mills capable of producing railroad rails – in Atlanta and Richmond – were concentrating on other war production. Locomotives were in such short supply that when J. E. B. Stuart captured a Yankee locomotive in one raid, the prize was dragged overland by horse and ox teams to Confederate lines. Even timbers for trestles and bridges were scarce.

The four bridges and several hundred feet of trestle on the Southern Railroad near Newton that were burned could be, and were, replaced, but only at the cost of forgoing new construction or repairs elsewhere. Grierson's raiders had also twisted the rails longitudinally as well as bending them. Even if they were reheated and straightened lengthwise, the twisting rendered the rail useless for guiding wheels. They were fit only for scrap – or perhaps as armor plating. Thus, these rails had to be replaced from dwindling stocks of spare rails or by cannibalizing little-used track. The damage on the New Orleans to Jackson railroad was so extensive that the line could not be used for the rest of the war.

The damage to rolling stock was also significant. The loss of two locomotives hurt, especially since one engine was capable of pulling 25 cars. Richardson's pursuit of Grierson had been delayed because the locomotive at Jackson was unable to pull a full load of cars. Grierson's Raid also deprived the Confederacy of nearly 100 railcars – left in ashes along sidings throughout Mississippi. These, along with the wagons destroyed or captured, further eroded the logistical capabilities of the South.

Another important success was the draft animals and slaves taken by the raiders. The Quinine Brigade and Hatch's and Grierson's forces returned to Union lines with a combined total of over 1,500 mules and horses and 1,200 freed slaves. The Confederacy would be deprived of the labor afforded by animals and men, while the Union gained them – especially as many ex-slaves joined the black regiments then forming. Finally, the Confederacy lost the services of hundreds of soldiers captured during the raid – both those carried into Union lines and those paroled throughout Mississippi.

Materiel tallies were not the raid's sole measure of success. Grant intended the raid as a diversion and it filled that purpose admirably. The raid's critics rightly point out that it failed to lure the garrisons out of either Vicksburg or Grand Gulf. None of the raid's planners expected that Pemberton would strip riverside garrisons to chase down a lone cavalry brigade. What was hoped for was that a deep raid would focus Pemberton's attention immediately before Grant's landing, and that reserves would be too busy chasing Grierson to reinforce against Grant's landing (as was then planned) at Grand Gulf.

The Confederate camps that Grierson's raiders destroyed denied Confederate soldiers shelter, reducing their effectiveness. A camp like the one pictured here provided troops with a place to sleep, rest, and eat shielded from sun and rain. (LOC)

On that score it succeeded splendidly. Buford's brigade of Loring's division – eight veteran infantry regiments – was being transferred back to Pemberton from Tennessee. The transfer was caused by Porter's running the batteries at Vicksburg, and the men were intended to reinforce the river garrison. Due to Grierson's Raid, the transfer was interrupted. The brigade's infantry spent two weeks futilely guarding the Gulf and Ohio Railroad against phantom Yankees instead of reinforcing Grand Gulf. Other regiments of Loring's division were moved from central Mississippi to cover the Southern Railroad. Finally, Pemberton sent most of what little cavalry remained under his command – including infantry mounted on spare horses – hunting Grierson in the week after Newton was raided. No cavalry was available to Pemberton and Bowen when Grant finally landed. The Confederates were blind when they most needed intelligence.

There was the morale impact of the raid. Grierson's Raid was an announcement that the Confederate monopoly on cavalry boldness was over. Union cavalry could equal and even exceed them. Grierson's seemingly

The 16-day raid often challenged the ingenuity of the participants in fixing meals. While food was obtainable from local sources, field kitchens had be abandoned with other baggage, requiring men to prepare their own meals, often with improvised utensils. (AC)

effortless ride through the heart of the Confederacy heartened the Union after a long, discouraging winter of failures. At the same time it made the South look foolish as its troops chased after will-o-wisps. Never mind that Grierson evaded his opposition using a combination of extraordinary skill, hard work, and good fortune. It looked effortless. While the Confederacy could seize on the failure of Streight's Raid – which took place at the same time – to salve their pride, Grierson's Raid was still humiliating.

While a detailed discussion of Streight's Raid lies outside this book, a comparison of the two raids highlights the factors that led to Grierson's success and Streight's failure.

Grierson was given troops appropriate for his task. He had three veteran cavalry regiments, each with over a year's worth of combat experience. They knew and were good at their trade. Streight was given four regiments of infantry, mounted for Streight's raid. Putting soldiers on horses does not make them cavalrymen. Infantry uses different tactics and weapons. The muzzle-loading infantry musket is of limited use on horseback, nor are infantry familiar with revolvers. Grierson's brigade had worked together as a team for several months prior to the raid, and each regiment knew and trusted the other regiments. Streight was given a composite brigade – units that had not fought together – and thrust immediately into combat. In a deep raid, unit cohesiveness counts.

Grierson traveled light. He had no baggage, and he had his men reduce their load to the absolute minimum needed for the fight. Although he expected the raid to take ten days, he carried enough rations for only five days. Grierson knew that food would be his for the taking, so there was no need to burden the horses by carrying extra. Streight brought tents, food, supplies, and extra ammunition with his raid. This required baggage wagons to accompany the cavalry, slowing Streight's movements.

Grierson's biggest gamble lay in the ammunition for the raid. His men carried only 40 rounds per weapon. This averaged 100 rounds per man – because most men carried multiple firearms, and some carried a few extra rounds – but it was enough for only two major battles. He could not reasonably expect to refresh his ammunition boxes from captured munitions. Had Grierson been pinned down near Newton, he could easily have exhausted his magazines and been forced to surrender. Hatch's Second Iowa, caught by Barteau's cavalry, fought a running battle from Palo Alto, Mississippi, back to Tennessee. By the time they reached the Union lines, most of the men were firing off their last rounds.

Yet the light loads increased Grierson's mobility. This reduced the chance that he would need to fight pitched battles. Grierson also understood that raiding was not about firefights. His job was to destroy a railroad – not fight enemy soldiers. A raid was about avoiding fights until you reached your targets, and striking at points where the enemy was absent, weak, or unprepared. The axe and the torch were the raiders' tools more than the carbine or saber.

Grierson was virtually unique among Union cavalrymen in this approach, repeating these tactics in a second, highly successful raid he led in 1864. Sooy

Smith brought a train on a raid that Smith led, and in which Grierson participated. Grierson advised leaving the baggage behind, but Smith ignored this counsel. As a result – and to Grierson's great frustration – Smith's Raid yielded only trivial success.

Speed and mobility was one key reason for Grierson's success. On a good day, Grierson's column averaged 40 miles. Even under absolutely wretched conditions – crossing the Noxubee bottoms in driving rain – the Yankee cavalry managed over 25 miles. When pushed, they achieved phenomenal distances. On the day they struck Newton, the brigade traveled over 40 miles, despite spending half a day destroying the railroad and facilities at Newton and the dozen miles around it. On May 1–2 they covered 76 miles without stopping. These speeds could not have been achieved had Grierson carried a baggage train. Certainly the Noxubee would have proved impenetrable to wagons. The artillery with Grierson was forced to break their guns and carriages into pack loads and carry them across the swamp on horseback and muleback. This would have been impossible with any type of artillery other than the light Woodruff gun.

Grierson's burst of speed on the last day was the reason that he escaped the enemy forces converging upon him. The day before, despite remaining in Summit until sunset, Grierson had pushed his men another 12 miles before stopping for the night. This frustrated one attempt to ambush him that night at Summit. The Confederate commander did not believe that Yankee cavalry could move so fast. By contrast, Streight was trapped by Forrest after stopping for the night, because Streight believed he was safe spending a night resting while in enemy territory.

Another factor contributing to Grierson's success was his ability to gather intelligence. A combination of the "Butternut Guerrillas" and runaway slaves gave Grierson outstanding situational awareness. He knew – not exactly, but with sufficient accuracy – what enemy forces were around and which were approaching. The ability of Yankee troops to pass themselves off as Confederates – done at numerous critical instances – gave Grierson a decisive edge over his pursuers. Slaves provided him with intelligence about the location of food stores and livestock that allowed Grierson to feed his men and to remount them on fresh animals. In turn, this allowed him to travel lightly and move fast.

Grierson compounded his knowledge of the enemy with his ability to deceive the Confederates about his intentions. He constantly threw off feints and side expeditions to confuse things. These did not always work. His detachment of 200 men on the fourth day of the raid – the Quinine Brigade – failed to lure Confederate cavalry away. But he detached the Second Iowa at a crucial moment, a deception that decoyed Barteau's cavalry away from the main body and on to a sideshow that took this group entirely out of the battle. The two diversions sent to Macon, Mississippi, on that same day – Forbes' company and the two riders sent to cut the telegraph line – succeeded beyond all expectation. They kept the Confederates focused guarding the Gulf and Ohio line to the point where the Southern Railroad was completely ignored.

Grierson also controlled the information that was going out about him. The first thing he did on entering a town was to secure the exits, to keep anyone from leaving to carry word of his presence. Often before leaving a town he would secure pledges of silence from the inhabitants. Were these pledges kept? Perhaps, but it mattered little. Grierson grabbed all of the best horses before leaving. The only beasts left for local Paul Reveres to ride were exhausted, lame, or infirm mounts. Nor was Grierson above misleading involuntary hosts about his intentions. At Garlandville Grierson let slip his intention to go to Enterprise – before heading in a different direction. At Union Church he allowed paroled prisoners to hear his plans to ride to Natchez, allowing one prisoner to "escape" unparoled – just to ensure that Wirt Adams would be decoyed.

Finally Grierson's decision to bring a battery of Woodruff guns paid off. These pieces were so weak as to be useless against any other type of artillery, but they were light and portable. The guns proved invaluable on two different occasions. The sole gun sent with Hatch facilitated the Second Iowa's escape from Barteau on April 21, and they proved the key to overcoming stubborn opposition when Grierson broke through the cordon tightening around him on May 1. In both cases the Confederates had no opposing artillery, and in both cases the guns proved most effective in panicking state or irregular troops. Without the Woodruff guns it is possible that either Hatch or Grierson might have been pinned down until Confederate reinforcements arrived.

The ability of Union troops to get intelligence and assistance from slaves contributed significantly to the success of both Grierson and Hatch during the raid. (LOC)

CONCLUSION

Grierson's success was based on good troops led by great commanders. Grierson was not the raid's only outstanding officer. Captain Forbes, Colonel Hatch, and Lieutenant Colonel Blackburn all turned in inspired performances. The margin of success was much narrower than it appears in retrospect, as Lieutenant Colonel Blackburn's first and fatal lapse illustrated. The raid's success was due in large part due to Grierson's shrewd judgment, and his ability to sense the right time to strike and the right time to run. The raid contributed both materially and strategically to Grant's ultimate victory at Vicksburg.

The raid also illustrated that the South was a hollow shell. A force that pierced the protective crust of Southern armies could move almost at will. Grierson would demonstrate that again in 1864 with a second successful raid through Mississippi. Sherman, one of Grierson's early supporters, drew the right lessons from Grierson's Raid and emulated it on a much larger scale in 1864 with the March to the Sea. As with Grierson, Sherman's army was able to march through the South's interior almost at will.

Good fortune and success followed many of the raid's participants over the course of the war. Both Hatch and Grierson were marked for higher command and after the war both men, despite a lack of formal military training, were offered regular army commissions, commanding the Ninth and Tenth US Cavalry – the famed Buffalo Soldiers – respectively. Henry Forbes was promoted to lieutenant colonel by the war's end, rising to second in command of the Seventh Illinois. His brother, Stephen Forbes, ended the war as a captain. Richard Surby survived his wound, and a stay at Libby Prison. He was exchanged in June 1863 with the other surviving Union prisoners of Grierson's Raid. He recovered his diary, and served with the Seventh Illinois Cavalry for the rest of the war. When the regiment's term of service expired in 1864, Surby reenlisted, and was promoted to regimental quartermaster.

Grierson and his men took no further part in Grant's Vicksburg campaign. Despite Grierson's efforts to rejoin Grant, transportation upriver

could not be arranged until after Vicksburg's fall. Nathaniel Banks, commanding the Army of the Gulf, attempted to operate on the principle of "finder's keepers" with the two cavalry regiments unexpectedly appearing in his department. He hung on to them until Port Hudson fell, in July 1863, reluctantly releasing them afterwards. He hated to let them go. They were not only good troops, they were lucky ones. Commanders hated losing lucky troops.

Despite its success, Grierson's Raid proved a nine-day wonder. In its aftermath it made Grierson a household name and his soldiers famous. Yet the romance that attached to Confederate cavalrymen failed to stick to Grierson's men. By the time the last Civil War veterans passed on, while the exploits of Stuart, Morgan, and Forrest – even Custer – were being talked about, Grierson's Raid was largely forgotten. Yet Grierson matched all of the Confederates, and far outperformed George Custer.

Benjamin Grierson and his officers relax at Baton Rouge after the raid. Grierson is probably the one on the far right, and Colonel Reuben Loomis may be the one with his hand on his face. (AC)

BIBLIOGRAPHY

Grierson's Raid made a major splash during the Civil War and the immediate years following. A diligent researcher can find news accounts that appeared in *Harpers*, the *New York Times*, and Frank Leslie's *Illustrated Weekly*. Some of these are online, and I was fortunate enough to find several to use.

The starting point for anyone interested in reading more about Grierson's Raid is Dee Brown's seminal *Grierson's Raid*, the book that rescued Benjamin Grierson and his brilliant raid from ill-deserved obscurity. While other book-length accounts of the raid have appeared since, it remains the standard work.

Beyond the usual suspects (the official records, *Battles and Leaders of the Civil War*, etc.) that provide background information and official documentation, three first-person accounts of the raid were written by participants. Sergeant Richard Surby had his account published at the war's end. Benjamin Grierson and Stephen Forbes both wrote works available only in manuscript form through the twentieth century. While Dee Brown was lucky enough to have access to all three, due to living close to the two unpublished works, I was luckier still. Both unpublished manuscripts were printed in the twenty-first century, which allowed me to read them without making a trip from Texas to Illinois. Forbes' account is in Volume 6 of *Battles and Leaders of the Civil War* (a modern continuation of the nineteenth-century series), and Grierson's memoirs appeared in book form in 2008.

Additional reading for the interested is William Leckie's biography of Grierson (which also covered his early years and postwar career as commander of the Tenth Cavalry) and Neil York's *Fiction as Fact*, which examines the raid and various treatments of it – both fact and fiction.

Grierson's Raid also formed the basis for Harold Sinclair's 1956 novel, *The Horse Soldiers*, which became a movie of the same name staring John Wayne in 1959. *The Horse Soldiers* – both the book and the movie – is only incidentally related to the actual events, as both works changed